breaking up

Kate Cann

Livewire

First published by Livewire Books, The Women's Press Ltd, 2001
A member of the Namara Group
34 Great Sutton Street, London EC1V 0LQ
www.the-womens-press.com

Reprinted 2001

British Library Cataloguing-in-Publication Data
A catalogue record for this book is available from the British Library.

ISBN 0 7043 4976 0

Typeset in 12/14pt Bembo by FiSH Books Ltd, London.
Printed and bound in Great Britain by Cox & Wyman Ltd,
Reading, Berkshire.

For my parents, who stayed together

breaking up

One

This Christmas was the worst, the foulest, the most horrible ever.

If there is an Anti-Christ, this was his Anti-Christmas. Thank God it's over. Thank God I'm back at school.

The only time over Christmas when we could half-way pretend things were half OK was when the telly was on. But then we had to watch seasonal adverts, didn't we. All those sparkly snowy firelit scenes of families going gaga with love at each other, making my family's angry, cold, desperate Christmas seem all the worse. Making all the tension and the pretence and the rows and the crying seem even more horrific. And doubling the huge, huge feeling of failure underneath it all, because we've failed at being happy. We're so far away from being happy like those glowing advert families we could be on another planet.

I don't want to think about it, not any more. I've had my head stuffed so full of it I'm sick of it. All the silences, broken up by Mum and Dad sniping at each other, and hearing Mum cry upstairs, and Dad shouting with all the veins in his neck standing out and his eyes like a madman's, and Mum throwing that half-full bottle of wine against the wall and storming out of the house and Dad's face closing in all bitter like a trap and my two little sisters creeping into my room saying 'Fliss – do Mummy and Daddy hate each other?' and me inventing all this cosy crap for them about it just being a bad patch when inside my guts were twisted up and knotted tight with fear and misery.

Don't want to think about it.

Christmas was shit and that's all there is to it.

The stupid thing is, though, Mum used to be so good at doing Christmas. We all had a great time. I have really happy memories from when I was little – going out to farms to buy holly, making snowmen scenes with cotton wool, baking special biscuits, hanging them from the tree, eating them when they fell off. She really liked the build-up – she never seemed to get stressed. And then first Alexa and then Phoebe got born, but it didn't spoil anything. She'd let me take charge – she'd tell me what a great helper I was. And when Dad got in from work she'd tell him how good I'd been and he'd look around at all the tinsel and holly and mess and just laugh, and pick me up and kiss me . . .

Don't want to think about that. Don't want to think about how different it is now. Think about Simon instead. It's Wednesday evening, so I'm off round his house. I always go round his house on Wednesday evenings. We've got so much work with our GCSEs coming up in the summer we agreed we'd only see each other once during the week, and Wednesday was the middle day.

We've been going out for five months, one week and four days. I'm already thinking what I can buy him for our six-month anniversary. Six months – that's a long time. If you've been with someone that long, you're really committed, aren't you?

As I walk up Simon's front path I'm hoping like I always hope that it'll be him and not his mum who answers the door. She's a nurse and she does all these odd shifts and you never know when she'll be around. Not that I don't like his mum, not exactly. She's always nice enough to me – she's soft-spoken Scottish and she seems kind. But Simon told me once that she thinks we're too young to get all 'serious' about each other. Funny how 'serious' in a Scottish accent sounds *really* serious. Simon's a bit younger than me, you see. He's not going to be sixteen for ages.

I always feel she's a little bit guarded with me, a little bit disapproving. If she picks up the phone to me more than once a night she'll say 'You again, Felicity?' Stuff like that.

But this time I'm in luck. The door swings back and Simon's there, grinning out at me, with his hair that always seems to need cutting all sticking up on top. He pulls me inside the door, and we go up the stairs hand in hand, him in front, me behind, and I love that feeling that he's taking me with him, I love that feeling that we're joined together, that I belong.

Once inside his room he pushes the door shut and puts his arms round me and we start kissing. We always do this.

One of the reasons is his mum doesn't like us being shut up in his room together and she's liable to just knock once on the door and come straight in and it's a bit embarrassing if you're in a clinch. But she never comes up right after I've just got there. I suppose it'd make her look too suspicious.

Simon isn't that brilliant at kissing. I know I'm the first girl he's been out with properly and I'm pretty sure he hasn't got off with too many before me. So I suppose really he just needs the practice. I wish he'd slow down, I wish he'd answer my kiss, answer me, not just stab his tongue around like it's looking for something it can't find. Last New Year's Eve, this guy I didn't even know gave me a kiss, and it was brilliant; it was slow, and he knew what he was doing, he took charge but he responded, too – he listened to me, somehow. It was over a year ago now but I still remember it.

'So how're you, Flissy?' says Simon. 'Isn't it 'orrible being back at the dump?'

I murmur 'Yeah', even though I'm glad to be back at school, glad to be away from all the shit at home, and I crane up towards his mouth again. Simon and I have this agreement that we don't act like girlfriend and boyfriend at school. Too many people take the piss out of you if you do. It's OK for couples like Dom and Hannah – they're so cool they can get away with anything. They were up before the Head at the end of last term for practically having it off in the Year Eleven girls' toilets.

Simon detaches himself from me, and wanders over to the other side of the room to put a CD on. Then we sit down side by side on the floor, leaning up against his bed. He puts his arm round me and I lean my head on his shoulder, which is how we always sit. Sometimes when we're sitting like that I feel so warm, so loved, the thought goes through my head that I could die right then and not care.

'At least I'll see a bit more of you now,' I say. 'I've hardly seen you over Christmas.'

'Yeah, well, you know what Christmas is like. Everyone came down. Uncle Fraser and everyone came down from Aberdeen and stayed for over a week.'

'What're your cousins like?' I ask. I stop myself adding 'I would've liked to meet them. Why didn't you ask me to meet them?'

'They're OK. It's stupid, we're always all distant and everything for the first few hours, all trying to impress each other, and then it's like we're kids again, you know, ganging up against the grown-ups, trying to get out of the washing up. Mike and Jamie slept in here.' He looks round his room, like he's savouring the memory. 'I was really pissed off at first, you know, them in my space, but it turned out great. We'd stay awake till three in the morning, just talking.'

'What on earth about?'

'Everything. What is reality. How do we know we're not just figments of each other's imagination. How computers are going to become so intelligent they'll outstrip man and maintain themselves and take over the running of everything and gradually man'll lose control of the planet and become extinct.'

'H'm. Long as woman doesn't,' I say, but he doesn't laugh. Just for a moment I'm feeling really jealous that he was talking about that kind of deep stuff with people other than me. Simon and me talk, you see, all the time, all about everything. It's our special thing, our bond together.

'Did you tell them you've got a girlfriend?' I ask.

'Yes,' he answers, but in a way that makes me think he didn't.

'You haven't asked me what kind of Christmas I had,' I say.

'Yes I have.'

'Not really. Only on the phone.'

There's a tiny pause, then he says, 'OK, tell me about it.'

I start to cry. I cry for a good minute or so, then I blow my nose and tell him all about our Christmas.

Two

I always feel better when I've been round to see Simon. Like I've had a long, warm, relaxing bath or something. He's so understanding, the way he lets me just spill it all out about Mum and Dad and everything. I can still remember the first time I cried in front of him, it was like this wall between us had collapsed, like I could really be myself with him, with no pretence. I'm always telling him how alone I'd feel if it wasn't for him.

As I go home on the bus I think about what he said, about how I need to put everything in perspective. He said think less about how your folks are together, more about how they are with you. He told me about this mate of his who's got an awful home life and he's really hoping his old man will leave home because he hates him so much. I'm luckier than that, Simon says, because I still love both my parents, and they're both good to me. And it's true, I guess. I do still love them. I s'pose I've got closer to Mum over the last few years, and Dad's got a bit grim and grey and cut-off. But I know he's still there for me. He's less moody than Mum; more fair, somehow.

I get back home at about nine-thirty. Mum's standing in the hall with a big bin bag. She looks up a bit guiltily, as if I've caught her out, then she says, 'Hello darling. Had a nice evening?'

'What you doing, Mum?' I ask.

'Oh, just chucking out some old decorations. We've got together so much over the years, I could hardly get it all back in the cupboard. I vowed to myself I'd have a clear-out before the end of the month.'

I walk over, peer into the bag. I can see ropes of tinsel, the little plastic snowmen we've had for as long as I can remember, the cardboard nativity scene I made in a shoebox when I was about seven.

'It's only the old tat,' says Mum. 'I've kept loads of other stuff.'

Suddenly, I can't bear for her to be chucking all of this out. It seems to put the seal on something, like we're never going to have another Christmas. I want to say something but my throat freezes and I can't. I'm willing Mum to talk, to say something about what a horrible time it's been, how it's going to get better, but she just bends down and ties up the bag. 'Where is everyone?' I ask.

'Dad's still not home; Alexa and Phoebe are in bed.'

'Oh. Well – I'm going up, Mum. I'm knackered.'

'OK, darling. G'night.'

I turn the light out as soon as I can and roll myself up tight in my duvet so I'm swaddled in it, so I can't move.

I think about Mum chucking out those old decorations to leave for the bin men. I think about how she's changed, how the house has changed.

I suppose she used to be the classic cosy Mum, there when you got in from school, making you some toast and a drink. She made ordinary days special. She'd plan outings and surprises – she'd cook feasts. She loved all the seasons, not just Christmas – she'd turn them into festivals. Soon as the daffs were out in the shops and the street markets she'd buy loads, fill flouncy, frilly, yellow jugfuls all over the house. Pancake Day was a competition – who can toss theirs the highest? And then Easter, we'd paint hens' eggs and do an egg hunt in the garden. Mum got up very early, just to hide loads of little foil-wrapped chocolate eggs in among the flowers and in the trees. She'd make a delicious breakfast and make Dad come out on the narrow terrace and eat it with her and watch us search.

All three of our birthdays are in November. Weird. My gran used to say, 'Don't you get fed up, dear? Three birthday parties all so close together.' And Mum would shake her head and laugh, and say it was the in-between bits that made her fed up.

It was, too. She used to get really moody if 'nothing was happening'. She wanted life to be one long festival, one long celebration. About six months ago her friend Jan persuaded her to turn all her party skills into a business, and they started up this little catering company together doing kids' parties. A lot of people would sooner have their teeth pulled with pliers than run a kid's party, especially for their own kid, so the new company gets quite a bit of business. But there isn't a great deal of money in tiny egg sarnies and party bags, and the company isn't turning a profit, despite the hours she puts into it. She and Dad fight about it all the time – he says it takes up too much of her energy for too little reward. She says it keeps her sane and there's no price on that.

Life's been different since her company started up, that's for sure. Hectic, chaotic. It makes Dad furious. Then she gets mad because he won't support her, and she gets cross with me, too, if I don't take her side. 'You're just like your father,' she says. I hate it when she does that. I know she means it nastily.

Sometimes, I get this babyish thought that I wish we were enough for her still. I wish everything at home still made her happy and she didn't need something outside. I know that's selfish.

I'm half asleep now, and my mind's bogged down in nostalgia with how it used to be . . . all Mum's seasons scrolling past . . . Halloween. That used to be brilliant – Mum's favourite time. She loved it long before the high street stores cottoned on to the money-spinner it was in the States, and started flogging witch hats and monster masks. We'd hollow out pumpkins, carve scary faces on them and put night-lights inside. The faces glowed orange even without their candles lit, like they were alive. They made me feel weird, kind of scared but happy too. Mum used to say it was OK to be a bit scared. Life is scary sometimes, she said. And there's got to be a dark side, or how would you know when it's light?

This memory floats up inside my head. Just after I'd started at secondary school she arranged a big bonfire party. She knew I found it all a big strain, being all grown up and capable at my new enormous school, so she arranged a party for half-term, so I could let rip a bit, she said. She and a couple of friends got together and built a huge bonfire on a bit of wasteland next to a closed-down factory. I remember Dad being grumpy about it and groaning on about how much time it took up, but Mum and her friends carried on, and they arranged who'd bring the drink and who'd bring the hot dogs, and everyone started to gather at about six, when it was dark. Most of the little kids had dressed up as witches and ghosts and stuff, and brought pumpkin lanterns, and someone had brought along a load of sparklers, and there was all this food, and people kept turning up and handing stuff round and having a good time.

It was great, the best party ever. A load of my mates from school were there and we all acted like little kids again, spooking ourselves, racing off into the dark and back again. And all the time the bonfire was getting brighter and hotter and more spectacular, and people were in this big ring all round it, completely drawn to it, just standing around scorching their faces and soaking it up. Mum came over and put her arm round my shoulders and said, 'D'you know why bats are associated with witches?'

'Cos they're yucky and scary?'

'More than that. When witches were being burnt at the stake, it was often at night. Insects would be drawn to the light of the fires. And then maybe a big bat would fly in close, grabbing the insects. And then shoot off fast because of the heat. People would see it fly away and say it was the soul of the witch, shape shifting. Leaving her old body behind and escaping.'

'Creepy,' I giggled, and I was just about to go off

and find my mates again when she murmured, 'Imagine that. Just changing yourself and flying away. *God*, how brilliant.'

I remember the fervour in her voice, the longing – it really upset me. Did she really want to fly away, or had she just got one of her moods on? I was troubled, but somehow I couldn't ask her about it. Later I saw her and Dad arguing because he wanted to leave the party and go home and she didn't. And it hit me like a blow that this was nothing unusual, that they hadn't been getting on that well for quite some time now.

But I pushed it down in my mind and forgot about it.

I can't forget about it now. It's like it's filling my brain. I know I won't ask her about it, though. I don't ask her about anything to do with Dad because that would make it real. Last year I'd've said there was nothing I couldn't discuss with Mum, nothing at all. It's all different now though. I'm so scared. I'm scared of her answer. I'm scared because I don't know what's going to happen.

Three

Thursday lunchtime, I'm mooching about bogged down by thoughts when Liz suddenly appears at my side. Liz is just about my closest friend apart from Simon, although since he and I got involved, my friendship with her has kind of lapsed. I still see her at school, but I hardly ever go out with her and everyone else at the weekends, so I can't really share in the gossip in the week.

She's the sort who has masses of close friends, though. She's OK about it. 'Come on,' she says, linking her arm through mine. 'Let's get out of here.'

'What – into town?'

'Yeah. The whole point about signing up as prefects was to get passes to get out at lunchtime, wasn't it?'

'Well...'

'Look – I've gotta get out of this dump. Come on. There's a new salad bar thingy opened up. Italian. Meg says it's good. Cheap, too.'

I pull open my bag, stalling. I'm pleased she's asked me, but I want to save my money for Saturday night, and going out with Simon. 'Well . . .' I say, 'I brought sandwiches today . . .'

She pounces, grabs the packet out of my hand. 'What are they? Cheese? We'll have those on the way down. Then I'll buy you a Coke. Oh, come on, Fliss – I never see you nowadays! There's Meg – let's go!'

And I find myself being chivvied towards the school gates, copping envious glances from a group of Year Tens as we sail through. '*Freedom!*' says Liz, making sure they all hear. 'Let's go!'

We hurry along the main road to where the shops start. Liz hands out my sandwiches. 'All right then, Fliss,' says Megan. 'How's the big romance going?'

'Fine,' I say, a bit guarded, because these two can tease you like anything when they're in the mood.

'Shagged him yet have you?' she demands, and Liz bursts out laughing, spraying cheese sandwich everywhere. I feel hurt but only for a second or so, then I'm laughing too.

'You mind your own business,' I say.

'That means you haven't,' crows Megan. 'You do know you're going to have to make the first move, don't you?'

'*No!* Just cos he's not always turning the pressure on, like the sex maniacs you go out with!'

Megan snorts, and Liz laughs. 'Baby-faced Simon,' she says. 'Aw. He still as soft on you as ever?'

'Softer,' I gloat. 'He's lovely. He's so *sweet*.'

'H'm. I wish Jake was sweet,' grumbles Megan. Megan doesn't exactly go out with Jake, she 'sees' him. He's nineteen, and he works late and owns a motorbike.

'Ach, you'd be bored with sweet, Meg,' says Liz. 'You know you would.'

'Well, I'm not bored,' I retort. 'Simon's just – I don't know. We just feel so right together. He's lovely.'

'God, Fliss – you want to get out more,' says Megan. 'Come out with us, Saturday!'

'I'm seeing Simon.'

'One night apart won't kill you. We're going to Club Nitrate.'

'Simon'd hate it if I went to a club on my own.'

'*Aaaagh!* You are doing my head in, Fliss! All this committed crap. Come out and have some fun! Remember when Club Nitrate opened?'

I start to laugh.

'And you got off with one of the bouncers?'

'He *wasn't*,' I squeal. 'He was his younger brother.'

'Whatever. We all got in for free the next time we went there!'

We've reached the new salad bar, and we pile in, still laughing. There's a twenty-something, dark-haired guy with a sleeveless T-shirt that shows off his muscles grinning at us from behind the counter. Megan gives this low whistle, under her breath. 'Ladies!' he says. 'Can I help you?'

'Um,' says Liz.

'We have four types of pasta salad, fresh coleslaw, green salad, tomato and basil salad, potato salad . . . three scoops, one pound ninety-five.'

We peer through the glass at the big trays of fresh-cut salad. It looks fabulous. 'We put it in these tubs here,' he says, picking one up and waving it at us.

'I'd like some of that coleslaw,' says Megan.

'Eat healthy, stay beautiful, hey?' he says, leering across at Megan, like he knows she's attracted to him.

'And some green salad – and some of that twirly pasta stuff there.'

'Dressing is free,' he adds encouragingly. 'So is the fork.'

At my side Liz is trying not to snort with laughter. She nudges me, then jerks her head at the huge phallic pepper grinder standing on the counter.

'You must have olives as well,' the guy's gushing. '*Ve-ry* Italian. Look – I'll add these on the house. Now – pepper?' And he picks up the huge grinder.

Five minutes later, we've found a bench in the tiny park nearby, and we're sitting side by side opening up our tubs of salad. 'Seriously, I thought I'd choke when he started jabbing that massive pepper pot across the counter at you,' Liz sniggers.

'I know,' says Megan. 'God – I hate olives.'

'Why didn't you tell him?'

'He'd've been hurt!' She scoops out the olives one by one and drops them on the ground. 'I reckon I'm in there. Want to go back tomorrow?'

'Oh God – are you on the pull again?'

'Yeah well – he was OK. And I'm pretty sure Jake's seeing someone else at the moment.'

I turn and look at her. 'Honestly, Megan – why d'you put up with it?'

'Cos Jake is fit. And cos that way I'm free too, aren't I?'

'Yeah, but you don't really want to be. You'd like to go out with Jake properly, wouldn't you?'

Megan shrugs, stares at the olives she's chucked on the ground. 'Get all tied down like you, you mean?'

'I'm *not* tied down. What we've got – it's special.'

'Yeah, OK.'

'We *trust* each other.'

'So if you trust each other so much, why can't you come out on your own sometimes? You never come out with us any more.'

'But it's different now! I want to be with *him*. You'd understand if you –'

'– fell in lurve?' finishes Megan, all sarky.

I shut down then, cut off from her, silent. Next to me, I can feel Liz jabbing her elbow into Megan's side. There's a pause, then Megan says, 'OK, OK. Look, Fliss – I'm glad it's working out for you. Honestly.'

'She's just jealous,' adds Liz, all appeasing.

There's an awkward silence. I know they think I'm prickly about Simon. He had this big crush on me for months, following me about, asking people about me, and it was a bit of a joke among our group, because he's younger, because he was seen as a bit of a nerd. Then he got up the courage to ask me out and everyone was dead amazed when I said yes. I was a bit amazed myself. But there was something so fantastic about the way he looked at me, the way he seemed so unconditionally in love with me...

'It's just – we miss you, you know?' says Liz, breaking into my thoughts. 'We miss how it used to be.'

I'm back from school a bit late on Thursday, because I have to go to the library and look something up about the rise of the Fascists in Germany. I've got an essay to do, one of the final bits of coursework, and I'm planning to make sure it's A Star material. Sometimes I can really get into my work. I like it because it's just me, no one else, and I can control it. I walk into the kitchen hoping things are OK and dinner won't be long but Mum greets me with 'Fliss! Thank God you're back! I've got to go in half an hour!'

I look around – the sink's piled high with saucepans and every kitchen surface is covered with big oval plates heaped with party food wrapped up in clingfilm. 'We've been asked to do the food for a leaving party!' Mum's chirping, all excited. 'You know – *adults*!'

She looks at me, eyes glowing. She and Jan have been trying to break in to the adult market for a while now. 'The caterers who were going to do it dropped out right at the last minute so the company phoned Jan and she said we could handle it!' she goes on. 'I've been working like a slave all day!'

'That's great, Mum!' I say. And it is great. Great to see her so happy anyway. Except it's to do with the outside again, isn't it. With getting away from us.

'It was pure chance. He saw that flyer we sent round and just phoned in desperation. And Jan said yes. If we pull this off – well, it's quite a big company. It could *make* us.'

'That's great,' I repeat. 'What d'you want me to do?'

'Just help me get this stuff out to the car. And then – d'you mind holding the fort for me again, darling?'

'Holding the fort' is Mum's term for taking care of Alexa and Phoebe. I feel this rush of self-pity. I've got a major essay to do. I want someone to take care of *me*.

'Sure,' I say. 'That's fine.'

And I help her load up the car, and wave her off. I feel kind of panicky as she drives away, like she really is escaping, flitting off like the Halloween bat. 'Don't be stupid,' I tell myself as I walk back into the hall. I can hear the girls squabbling in front of the telly in the back room. I think about going into the messy kitchen, clearing it up and rooting around for something to feed them on. And suddenly, out of the blue, I get that feeling again, that feeling that started at Christmas when everything was so hideous, like I want to scream and scream only I can't, it can't come out, it's there bunched in my throat like a fist.

I walk into our little front room and pick up the phone and dial Simon's number. His mum answers after three rings and I ask to speak to Simon.

'Simon? That's Felicity is it?'

'Yeah,' I mumble.

'Good grief, didn't you get enough of him at school?' she asks, all jolly, but you can tell she's irritated underneath.

I don't say anything, I can't, and I hear the sound of the receiver being banged down on the table. Then Simon's voice says, 'Hello?'

I can't answer. I can't speak to him. Just the sound of his voice makes my throat give way.

'Fliss? What is it? What's up?'

'It's . . . it's . . .'

'Jesus, what is it?'

'Nothing,' I gulp. 'Just – Mum's got to go out, and she's leaving me to do the clearing up and make the dinner and –'

'Christ, Fliss, is that all? I thought something was really wrong!'

'It *is*!' I wail. 'I feel horrible. I can't bear it! It's like Mum's just switched off from us. Like all she cares about is her catering company. She doesn't give a shit about my exams.'

'Oh, come on, Fliss. Of course she does.'

'She *doesn't*. It's just her company! And what scares me is if she makes a real go of it, makes enough money, she'll leave. She'll just walk out.'

This comes out of my mouth like I've suddenly been possessed. I've never, ever thought this before. But as soon as I say it I know it could be true.

And I wanted to make Simon take me seriously, and saying that's enough.

'Oh, come on, Flissy,' he says, all gentle. 'She's not going to leave.'

'She just wants out. I know she does.'

'From your dad, maybe, but not from you and your sisters.'

'But he'll never leave. He just . . . wouldn't. He stays late at the office and everything but he always comes home. She'd have to leave him. Oh *God*. These last weeks – they've been getting on worse than ever.'

Simon listens while I tell him about the row I overheard the other night, while I tell him about how the only time Mum smiles is when she's getting away from the house. 'I can't bear it,' I say. 'It's my GCSE year. I need *support*.'

And then he says the words I've been hungering for: 'You have got support, Flissy. You've got me, haven't you?'

Four

Simon's words are like a fix. They get me through the next hour and a half or so. I clear up, then I make the girls come in and help dry the pots, then I let them watch telly again while I make them beans on cheese on toast. They ask for pudding so I find a KitKat and split it between them, and slice up a large apple. You can tell they're not that impressed by their tea but they know better than to complain.

'Will Mum bring home any leftovers?' asks Phoebe. 'From the party? For supper?'

'Nothing you'd like,' I snap. 'It's not that kind of a party.'

We finish eating in silence, then I make them help clear the table, then I tell them it's bedtime.

'Do we need a bath?' asks Phoebe.

'How the hell should I know?' I say. 'Just clean your teeth and get to bed.'

21

I watch them plod upstairs and I feel bad for a minute, sorry for them, then I feel this rush of anger against Mum again. They're her kids, not mine. I'm tired. Drained with resentment. It's nearly nine o'clock and I just want to get to bed myself.

'Fli – iss!' It's Alexa, calling down the stairs.

'What is it?'

'I've got baked beans down my sweatshirt.'

'So? Bung it in the dirty clothes basket.'

'It's my *school* sweatshirt. And I haven't got a clean one. I've just looked.'

'Well what d'you expect me to do about it?'

There's a silence, then Alexa repeats, close to tears, 'It's my *school* sweatshirt. I need it for tomorrow.'

Again, that great gush of self-pity, enough to wallow in, enough to drown in. I make myself breathe, deep, slow. Then I croak: 'Chuck it down. I'll sort it.'

Alexa lobs the sweatshirt down and I go up three stairs to collect it. 'Thank you, Flissy!' she quavers. She sounds so upset, I get this urge to run the rest of the way up and give her a hug, give her some comfort before she climbs into bed. Poor little sod, she knows what's going on, same as I do. She's full of fear too. But we can't share it, not any more, not after that dreadful Christmas. Can't admit anything's wrong. It's like monsters in the dark, behind the door, under the bed, when you're young. It's dangerous to name them. If you say they're there, they're there.

I turn round, go back downstairs. 'Night!' I call out coldly.

'Night!' she whispers back.

★

22

I head back to the kitchen, yank open the door on the washing machine, find it's full of white towels and sheets. I pull them out and dump them on the floor because they'll turn pink if they're washed with Alexa's purple sweatshirt. Then I add the soap and get this housewifely stab of guilt about running a wash just for one sweatshirt. So I stamp upstairs again and tip out the dirty clothes basket that stands on the landing and grab all the dark stuff I can. As I go by the girls' room, I can hear them whispering together. Phoebe sounds likes she's crying. 'Great, Mum,' I think savagely. '*Great.*'

I load the machine, turn it on, then I put the kettle on. It's nine-fifteen. Too late to start work. Shit – this whole evening has been wasted. I'm going to bed. Except I can't. I've got to stay up and wait for the wash to finish and put Alexa's stupid sweatshirt in the drier, because there won't be enough time to dry it in the morning. I could leave a note for Mum, I suppose. Or Dad. Except if they're really late, and miss it, it'll still be soaking wet in the morning and Alexa will freak and . . .

I feel so screwed up, so lousy I can't move. I wouldn't mind helping out if everything was OK, I really wouldn't. But what's the point of all this – of washing up and clearing away and looking after the girls – if our family's being destroyed? It's like tidying the house before an earthquake. I stand there as the kettle clicks off and the steam from the spout fades away. I don't know how long I stand there. I feel like I can't move.

Then there's the sound of a key in the door. And Mum doesn't shout 'Hell-ooo' like she always does, so it must be Dad. I get this impulse to run out to him, like I used to do when I was little, but I don't. I flick the kettle on again and stay leaning against the counter, waiting.

'Here on your own?' he says, as he walks into the kitchen.

'Yeah. Mum got an evening job. A leaving party.'

'What're all these sheets doing on the floor?'

'I had to empty the machine. Alexa's sweatshirt needed washing.'

He doesn't say anything, just walks over to the fridge and pulls out a can of beer. Then he gets a glass down from the cupboard and transfers the beer to the glass. Slow, particular, absorbed. I watch him, vaguely repulsed.

I can't imagine my dad ever having sex. I mean – I know that's something no one wants to do, imagine your parents at it, because it's plain disgusting. But my dad's worse. He's grown into the sort of man you can barely even imagine having a body. Like his head's attached to some kind of thin, dry machine inside his suit. His suit's like his shell. Or his exoskeleton, like a beetle. He might just collapse without it.

Mum's so different. She's full of life. She kind of jokes and flirts with everyone; she lights up when someone new comes along. I can imagine her having sex all right, just not with my dad.

Maybe that's the problem.

'So you've been in charge have you?' he asks. He's not really interested though. He doesn't look at me – his eyes are flicking round the kitchen.

'Yes,' I say. 'I got the girls their tea. Beans on toast.'

I want him to say well done, I want him to meet my eye and say 'Look, don't worry, Fliss, Mum and I are sorting it out', but he doesn't. 'Beans on toast?' he echoes, all sarcastic and disapproving. '*Very* nutritious.'

'Well I didn't have time to do anything more,' I snap. 'I had to clear up the kitchen, and put the washing on, and –'

'What time did she go out?'

'I dunno. A couple of hours ago. I was supposed to do an essay tonight, but it's too late now.'

'It's not even ten o'clock yet.'

His lack of sympathy hits me; I can feel my eyes welling up with tears. 'I'm tired,' I say. 'We've got a load of work on at the moment, what with coursework and everything, and –'

'You haven't got the time to help out at home too, is that it? Plenty of people have to do both, Felicity.'

'And plenty of others get a lot more support than I'm getting at the moment!' I fire back.

I'm not a bit prepared for what happens next. Not a bit.

He turns on me, like he's focusing on me for the first time, and spits, 'Don't you say we don't support you! *We* support you! All this –' he waves his arm round at the kitchen – 'this is supporting you!'

'No it's not,' I croak. 'It's just shelter and food – it's not real support.'

And his face screws up and it's like he flips out completely. 'Not real support? *God*! You *selfish* little cow! You're self-obsessed! Your exams aren't everything, you know! They're not the *whole bloody world*!'

I'm so shocked, so hurt, I don't cry, I don't even blink. I just stare at him.

'All you can think about is yourself, isn't it? How this *shit* that's happening between me and Mum affects you. You don't think of your sisters, you don't think . . . *look* at you – you don't care!'

25

I can't move, I can't speak, I just watch him. He's staring down at the floor now, breathing hard, fists bunched. There's a long, long pause.

'Sorry,' he mutters. 'I – look, sorry.'

'I *do* care,' I whisper. 'I care more than anything. It's horrible.'

He doesn't answer me. We've crossed over the line, haven't we, I think. He's cracked. He's cracked and he's started being honest and even if it means naming the monsters and making them real we've got to do it, we've got to talk about it now.

'What are you going to do?' I breathe. 'You and Mum? Are you going to split up?'

He shrugs furiously, keeps staring at the floor.

'You should *talk* to her,' I go on. 'You should try and work it out. You could – you could go to a counsellor. Or there's a place called Relate, it –'

'It's gone past that,' he mutters.

'Don't say that!' I plead. 'Look – I know you row about her new company. But it's good, really. She's really happy about it.'

'Really happy to be away from here. No one ever knows if they'll get fed or if they've got clean clothes to put on in the morning – the bathroom hasn't been cleaned for weeks –'

'But that doesn't matter, does it?' I say eagerly. 'I'll do it. I wouldn't mind.' I wouldn't either. Not if everything else was OK and the only problem was the bathroom not getting cleaned.

But Dad sighs, and says, 'Look – it's not just her work, Felicity. Or the mess in the house. I'm not *that* trivial. We just don't get on any more.'

'But it's just a bad patch,' I mutter, and I realise I'm using the same lying words to him as I use to the girls.

There's another long silence. Dad heaves another sigh like he's dredging it up from his shoes. Then he starts to walk towards the door, saying, 'I'm going up. Got an early start tomorrow.'

As he passes me he pats me awkwardly on the shoulder and mutters, 'I'm sorry, Felicity. I'm sorry.'

I hate hearing that. I think I prefer him shouting at me.

Five

The next day as I walk into school I'm full of fear, frozen with it. I need Simon like an addict needs her next fix, I need him to make me feel better, human even, I need to see him just so I can get through the day. And so I can face going home again. All through registration and the first two lessons I'm sitting on all the horror inside me, pushing it down, promising it I'll sort it, soon as I see Simon I'll sort it.

The minute the buzzer goes for break I shoot to my feet and head for the door.

'Hey – Fliss?' Liz calls after me.

'Yeah?' I snap.

'Where you off to?'

'I'm trying to find Simon.'

'It's just – you look awful. You all right?'

'Yeah. No. Parents – you know.'

'Is it still as bad?'

'Worse.'

There's a little gap then, as if she's wondering what to say, and just as she opens her mouth to speak I gasp 'Gotta go, OK?' and disappear out the door.

And I'm off down the corridor, bulling my way through the crowds of kids. Once I would've told Liz all about it, but it's different now. Now nothing matters but finding Simon. I go out the main doors, round the corner to the Sports Hall, down the side where the smokers hang out, but I can't see him. I check my watch – break's halfway gone already. Where the hell is he?

I search and search but I don't catch sight of him until break's over, and everyone's surging through the big double doors again. It's him, it's definitely his back view, that's his hair all sticking up. But I can't get to him. I can't force my way through all these people before he disappears inside.

'Hey – SIMON!' I shout, over all the heads, my voice sounding shrill and desperate.

'Hey – SIMON!' some bloke echoes, his voice a mocking soprano.

Simon turns. I can tell even from this distance he's embarrassed. A couple of his mates are with him, grinning, watching him. I wave madly. He lifts his hand to half-mast. Waves reluctantly back.

'I gotta see you!' I shout. 'Lunchtime!'

'Ooooh, Simon, Simon, I gotta SEE you,' the same bloke mocks.

Simon nods, and turns away, very fast. I bet he's gone red. He hates it when something happens to make him go red. Well, I can't help that.

I feel calmer in the next lesson, knowing I'm going to meet Simon. If we're going out somewhere together after school, we always meet by the side gates. At lunchtime, soon as I can escape, I hurry over there.

He's not there, but I'm early, and I know he'll come. I wait for a couple of minutes, then I spot him walking towards me. He doesn't swagger, like most of the Year Eleven boys do. He's got this loping, gentle sort of walk. Kind of apologetic. Sometimes it irritates me but today it's all I want to see.

'Simon!' I call out, and I'm over in front of him, reaching my arms up round his neck.

'Hey – steady,' he mutters, getting hold of my hands, pulling them down. 'What's up?'

'I just needed to see you,' I say. 'That OK?'

'Well – yeah. Except – the way you shouted out over everyone –'

'Oh, why d'you care so much what other people think?'

His face grows sullen. I've touched a nerve, touched it deliberately. Simon is paranoid about looking like a fool in front of people. Even more paranoid than most kids.

I lace my fingers through his, pull him over to a vacant bench nearby. It's half shielded by a straggly bush and it's just about the nearest thing to privacy you can get in these grounds. 'Sorry,' I say. 'Sorry if I showed you up. It's just – aren't you getting a bit sick of not spending any time together inside school? I mean – we could have lunch together, we could –'

'But we *agreed*,' he says, still all sullen. 'You just get the piss ripped out of you in this place if you go around arm in arm.'

'You care too much about what other people think!'

31

'Yeah, yeah, so you said.'

'Well you *do*!'

'Yeah, you said.'

I don't like the way the conversation's going. I don't like the cut-off look on Simon's face. I cuddle up close to him, and say, 'OK, OK, sorry. It's just – it's been one of the worst weeks ever. It really has. I'm all on edge.'

He doesn't answer, so I press a bit closer and say, 'I need to get away, Simon. I really do. D'you want to take the bus out to the coast tomorrow? Whitness, maybe. We could make an early start . . . and get fish and chips in one of those grotty cafes . . .'

'They won't be open,' he says, unenthusiastically. 'It's winter.'

'OK, OK, we'll take sarnies. I'll bring 'em. And a flask of tea.'

'I said I'd meet the guys tomorrow. We were going to go into town. Max needs a new jacket.'

'Oh, great. And he absolutely needs you to help him choose it, does he?'

'No –'

'So come out with me instead.'

Simon pulls away from me, folds his arms, stares ahead of him. He's no good when we argue. He can never think what to say so I always win.

'Look, Fliss,' he mutters, 'ever since we've been going out we've seen each other in the *evening*, not the day. Well – Sundays sometimes. But not *Saturdays*.'

'I know,' I say. I quite liked that system when we started off together. It made me feel safe, like I knew where I was. But now . . . 'We're getting in a rut,' I say. 'Don't you want to do something different?'

'I've arranged to meet Max,' he repeats stubbornly. 'And the others. We're going back to Tom's after, to watch the match.'

I don't say anything. He *has* to spend the day with me, he *has* to. I stare ahead of me at the ground, and two fat tears slide down my face. 'They're splitting up, Simon,' I mutter. 'It's definite.'

'Oh – God. Oh – Fliss.' He puts an arm round me, pulls me against his shoulder. 'Oh, God – that's awful. They told you, did they?'

'Dad did.'

'What – without your mum there?'

'He just kind of – let it slip. He said it had gone past talking and counsellors and everything.'

'Will you tell your mum what he said?'

'I dunno.'

'So he said they were definitely splitting up?'

'Well – not in so many words, but –'

Simon sits back on the bench, pushing me off him just a little. 'It's when they *announce* it that you've got to worry, Fliss. I mean – he could just be letting off steam. Until they make the big decision, it could still get turned around...'

'This won't get turned around,' I sob. I hate saying that, because I feel like I'm jinxing us, jinxing the whole family, but I've got to make Simon see how serious it all is, how shitty I feel. 'It's horrible at home, Si. Really *horrible*. That's why I wanted to get out to the sea. I've got this thing that I really want to see the sea.'

Simon squeezes my shoulder, and rocks me a bit, then he says, 'OK, let's go to the coast for the day. We can get to the bus station by ten o'clock, yeah? I think the ones to Whitness are on the hour, aren't they?'

'The hour and the half hour,' I say. 'Oh, Si – d'you really want to go?'

'Yeah, yeah, it'll be great. We can have a whole day there.'

'You sure you want to?'

'Yes, Fliss – I've said I do!'

The buzzer's going for the end of lunch. We both stand up, and he gives me a quick hug, but we don't kiss. 'What about tonight?' I whisper. 'You want to do something tonight?'

'Well – if I'm skanking the guys tomorrow, maybe I'll hang out with them tonight. You know.'

'Why d'you feel you've got to make it up to them? Won't they understand if you say you're seeing me?'

'Yeah – yeah. Course they will. But – you know. I'd like to see them.'

'What – more than me?'

'Hey, Fliss – come *on*. I'm gonna be with you all Saturday.'

I bite back what I want to say. Which is: 'I mean it – more than me?'

Back when we first started going out, when we couldn't believe how good it was that we thought the same on so many different things, we agreed that jealousy and possessiveness were right out of order. 'If you really like someone,' we'd said to each other, 'you don't want to tie them down, make them feel bad. You want them to be free.'

I don't think I think that way any more.

'It's just – they'll be really pissed off I'm not watching the match with them, Saturday,' he goes on. 'So I ought to see them tonight.'

I leave a silence, and he says, 'That OK, Fliss? I won't go for long, just a couple of hours. We've got to be up early, right? Catch the coast-road bus!'

The last buzzer goes, and I say, 'Well don't drink too much tonight, OK?' I know they usually club together, get a load of lagers in. Max buys it, because he looks a lot older than the rest of them.

'Where would I get the money from to drink too much, eh?'

I make myself smile at him. 'OK, then. See you tomorrow at the bus station?'

'Yup,' he goes. 'Ten o'clock.'

'Don't let me down,' I say, and we both go back into school.

Six

It's grey and stormy the next morning. As I fill the flask and make the sandwiches the wind's chucking rain against the kitchen window and every time there's a fresh gust I jump. I'm on edge for the phone to go and it to be Simon wanting to cancel the trip on account of the weather.

As soon as I've shoved everything into my backpack, I leave for the bus station. I'll be early, but I can't stand being in the house waiting for the phone to ring. I feel better once I'm walking down the road. If he phones now, wanting to cry off, I won't be there, will I? Then he'll have to come and meet me. He'd never just stand me up.

It's still windy but I swear the rain's easing up.

It's only twenty to ten when I get to the bus station. There's a mucky little cafe there, run by a depressed-looking woman with dyed black hair, far too black for her white face. It's awful inside, all Formica and hard lighting, but it's better than standing around outside with the wind knifing through you. I order a mug of tea, add a big spoonful of sugar, and sit down by the window to wait.

Even though I'm sitting in this hole, it feels so good to be on route to somewhere different. And so good not to have to go back home for the rest of the day.

Saturdays used to be easy and relaxed in our house, full of potential, of different things happening, different people coming and going. Now Saturdays are battle-grounds. With silent, frozen wastes in between. It feels like it'll take for ever, just getting through a Saturday at home. It's only OK when either Mum or Dad is out of the house, and then the other one seems to come alive a bit, and suggests getting fish and chips or watching a film all together on the sofa.

It's nearly ten past ten and my mug of tea is mostly drunk and stone cold by the time Simon raps on the cafe window. He's sodden; rain's dripping off his scuzzy old cagoule. I'm half angry that he's late, half so glad to see him I don't care. I hurry out of the door and practically crash into him.

'I know I'm late!' he says, before I can accuse him. 'I was phoning you. I thought there's no way she'll want to go in this.'

'It's gonna brighten up,' I say, looking up at the gun-metal sky. 'I heard a weather report.' I don't know why I say that, because I didn't, but I need to convince him, I need to convince both of us.

'How come you left so early?' he moans.

'*Early?* This isn't early. Being up at eight in the morning making sandwiches and tea is early.'

'You didn't!' he scoffs.

'I did,' I say, and point at my backpack. Although actually I was up at seven in the morning because I couldn't sleep. My stomach was in a knot of fear and worry so I went downstairs to get a drink. The living room door was closed and through it I could hear Dad snoring quietly and I knew he and Mum had spent another night apart.

'What's in the sarnies?' asks Simon, grumpily.

'Tuna and tomato, and cheese and mayo.'

'H'm. We're gonna *freeze* in this wind, Fliss.'

'No we won't. It'll be great. It'll be – what's that word – bracing. And the beach'll be practically empty.'

'You're right there. No one else'd be stupid enough to go down there on a day like this.'

'OK Simon – we won't go then! You're just saying all this so you can go back to your mates!'

'No I'm not!'

'Well why are you being so miserable about it then?'

'I'm just cold.'

'Do you want to go or not?' I demand.

He looks down at the ground for a few seconds, then he mutters, 'No, it's OK. Come on.'

'Only I don't want to go if you're going to be all miserable the whole time!'

'I'm not. Come on, let's find the bus.'

'We've missed the ten o'clock one. We've got over fifteen minutes to wait now.'

'Don't grouse, Fliss. It'll just give it longer to stop raining, won't it?'

We hardly say anything to each other as we wait under the flimsy bus shelter with the wind scything at our legs.

He's right, it is stupid to go to the coast on a day like this, but I *have* to, I just have to, and I can't bear it that Simon doesn't understand that, that all he cares about is keeping warm and dry. After about five minutes he asks me if I saw some film or other that was on last night, and I snap, 'No. I was in my room with the music up so I didn't hear Mum and Dad fighting,' and he shuts up after that.

Once we're on the bus, though, tucked away at the back, seated side by side, we both feel a lot better. Simon's cuddling really close to me, trying to get warm, and I cuddle him back, and we're smiling now, and he goes, 'Sorry I was late' again. Soon we're away from the town and heading out along the coast. We look out at the bleak rain-lashed landscape and Simon says, 'Blimey, I'm glad I'm in here, aren't you?' and I laugh and pull out the flask and pour us half a cup of sweet tea. Then we share it, mouths close, breathing in the steam, giggling like idiots as the bus swerves on the bends and we try not to spill any.

It's hard, getting off the bus. If the wind was bitter in town it's savage here. But it's brilliant too. It's whipping my hair about and dashing great grey spumes of sea up against the wall in the little harbour. The gulls are surfing on the air, screaming with anger.

'Come on,' I shout, above the boom of the waves. 'Let's get down on the beach.' I grab Simon's hand and we make our way down the steep stone steps. The tide's on the way out, and once you get past the harbour there's a wide strip of pebbly shoreline, stretching away far as you can see. 'Let's get right down to the sea!' I say, and he grins at me, his nose already red with the cold, wanting to show he's up for this. We plough forward across the shingle to where the waves are chopping and breaking on the beach.

It's brilliant. It's what I needed, to stand here like this. I look out across the great grey span of water, pocked by the rain, rucked by the wind, surging up and down with the movement of the waves. I watch the shushing of the waves as they break on the shore, and the tightness inside me relaxes its hold just a bit and I hear myself breathing. Then I worm my way under Simon's arm and say, 'Shall we start walking?'

He looks down and kisses me, murmurs, 'You taste of salt.' We start plodding forward, heads down into the wind. The sound of the waves and the wind are filling my head, and there's no need to talk.

'Where exactly are we going?' asks Simon, after a while.

'Dunno. To the edge of the earth. Like the old maps. Then we'll fall off.'

'It's freezing!' he complains. But he keeps his arm round me, and we keep walking, on towards the cliffs rising up in front of us. My face feels flayed. My lips feel like they've been iced. But I keep walking.

We reach the cliffs; the shoreline dips back behind them, and there's immediate shelter from the wind as we follow it. 'Oh, God,' mutters Simon. 'What a relief.'

I don't like it as much. I miss the intensity of being out on the headland. But I'm pleased he's pleased.

'Can we stop and have those sarnies you made?' he asks.

'Simon! It's not even twelve o'clock yet!'

'I know, but I'm starving. I hardly got breakfast. Just a banana. Cos I was late.'

'Well, that's your fault.'

'Your fault you mean! For leaving your house so early!'

I pull up short and glare at him. 'You saying you wish

I hadn't? You saying you wish you could've got hold of me, and cancelled this?'

'No,' he says, half joking, half like he's sick of me nagging. 'Come on — let's find somewhere to sit down and have some tea at least. I need to thaw out.'

We walk on. Because it's far more sheltered this side of the cliff, it's used a lot more. You can tell. All along the flotsam line, where the sea's stopped coming in, there's a line of plastic bags and bottles and rubbish.

'Look at that,' I say. 'Isn't it horrible?'

'Yeah,' says Simon, disinterested.

'You know what I'd like to do? I'd like to get a really big Hoover, an industrial Hoover, one of those ones you can sit on, and I'd like to drive it along this beach and hoover up all that plastic crap.'

'You'd hoover up all the crabs too.'

'No I wouldn't. It'd have, like, this sensor on it that made it only suck up plastic. God, wouldn't that be so brilliant? Just to get rid of all the rubbish, on all the beaches everywhere. It's a real threat to the marine life, you know, plastic. It doesn't break down, and if seabirds and so on mistake it for food they could die, they could get poisoned or choke or something...'

Simon isn't listening. I'm boring him. When we first got together, if I'd gone into a flight of fancy like that, he'd've joined in with me, he'd've added to it, elaborated on it. That was one of the reasons I liked him so much, because he cared about nature and ecology and stuff. But now he's just looking for a good spot to have his tea.

'Look — over there,' he goes. 'By that big rock. That'll be sheltered.'

The sand's still damp when we sit on it, but neither of

42

us says anything. I pull out the flask and pour out a cup of tea, then I hand it to him.

He hunches over it, resigned. 'The rain's getting going again.'

'OK,' I say, and I can feel my throat tightening up again, like it's waiting to choke me. It's gone wrong, the whole day's gone wrong. 'Let's have this, and the sandwiches, and head back. Yeah?'

There's a tiny pause, then he mutters, 'You sure you don't mind?'

In answer I rip open the bag with the sandwiches in, hand one to him, and start stuffing another into my mouth. I don't feel a bit hungry, but I've got to pretend I'm OK, I've got to pretend things are going the way I want them to.

'I mean – if you want to see some more of the sea, we can go on, Fliss. What is it with the sea, anyway?'

I shake my head, chewing. I think I might start crying if I try to explain that to him, and I think he's getting tired of me crying.

And then it really starts to rain. Sheeting down, buckets of it. We press ourselves back against the rock, but there's no real shelter to be had. Raindrops ricochet like bullets off the rock face, hitting our faces.

'Oh, Jesus,' groans Simon. 'Come on, let's leg it.'

As we struggle back along the shoreline, I'm filled with the same hopeless sense of failure I had at Christmas. Other people would've made this a fantastic trip, a romantic trip. It wouldn't've rained – or if it had rained, they'd've enjoyed it, made it fun, somehow. Rushed back along the edge of the sea hand in hand and laughing. Been happy.

We're not happy. Simon's face is screwed up and ugly

43

as the rain knives down on him. The whole thing's been a failure. I know he's thinking – I could be warm and dry and watching the footie right now.

It takes us twenty minutes to struggle back up to the harbour. There's a scruffy, rundown pub on the other side of the road opened up for lunchtime. It's all lit up inside – it looks warm. 'Shall we?' says Simon.

I shake my head. I know they'll refuse to serve us because we're under age and it'll be just one more humiliation and I couldn't bear it. 'We're too wet,' I croak. 'Let's get to the bus stop.'

We have to wait nearly twenty minutes for the bus to take us back. We start to hold hands but it's so cold we end up tucking them in our pockets. I wait till we're sat down on the bus and I mutter, 'Look – I'm sorry. I just really wanted to see the sea. You know.'

'Well, you saw it.'

'Yeah. Thanks.'

We ride on in silence. It's not cosy like it was on the way out here, because we're just so wet and uncomfortable. Simon sneezes twice and says, 'If I've caught a chill and die it'll be all your fault,' and I try to laugh but it doesn't come out right.

When we get back to the bus station we have to go in different directions to get home. Simon says goodbye to me really quickly, hardly even kissing me, and I know it's because he's going to race off to Tom's house and see if his mates are still there. I want him to ask to see me that night, but he doesn't, he just says, 'Get home and get in a hot bath, Fliss, yeah? I'll phone, OK?' and hurries away.

Seven

I let myself in the front door and Mum comes dashing out of the kitchen and says, 'Fliss! You are absolutely *soaking*! Look at you – you're shivering! Come on – get out of those wet things – I'll go and run a hot bath for you.'

She helps me pull off my coat and then she dashes upstairs and I hear the water running. It's nice, it's like being a kid again, getting fussed over. Except there's a stone inside my stomach and I'm not sure where it's from any more – from her and Dad, or me and Simon, or just everything. 'D'you want some hot chocolate?' she asks, as she comes back down the stairs. 'You can drink it in the bath. I'll bring it up. Leave the door unlocked.'

I'm up to my chin in vanilla-scented bubbles trying to make my muscles relax when Mum comes into the bathroom with two mugs. She hands one to me, then puts the lid down on the toilet and plonks herself down. 'So how are you, Flissy?' she asks, taking a sip from her mug.

I sink back into the water and think of all the things I could say to her. 'All right,' I mutter.

'You and Simon getting on?'

'Yeah.'

'We don't see him much nowadays.'

Well, I don't want to ask him round to this war zone do I? I think, and Mum laughs sadly like she's read my mind, and says, 'I know it's been difficult recently.'

'That's an understatement,' I blurt out.

'I know, I know. OK, it's been awful. But – look – it'll get better.'

'Will it?' I want to believe her, I really do. I want to tell her what Dad said, that he thinks it's too late for them to put things right. I want her to tell me that's rubbish.

I look across at her, and I notice for the first time the dark rings under her eyes, the way her mouth's set hard. She takes in a deep breath, and says, 'Yes, it will. We're just – adjusting. To me working and stuff. I really want to get this company going, and Dad – I don't feel Dad's giving me much support.'

'But he gets back so late. From work.'

'Oh, I know he works hard. I mean – God – he tells me often enough. It's not like I expect him to start doing all the domestic stuff or anything. Just to pull his weight a bit more. Or at the very least, not create this bloody atmosphere all the time, as if I'm failing everyone just cos the kitchen's a tip or we've run out of milk...' She pauses, looks across at me, manages a wan smile. 'Sorry. I shouldn't be moaning on like this to you. I just thought – I wanted to have a talk with you. You know.'

46

I take a deep breath, and remember the way Dad was the other night, the way he flipped, and mutter, 'It's not just you working, though, is it, Mum?'

'What d'you mean?'

'I mean – you and Dad hardly seem to get on about anything. Nowadays.'

She's started rocking herself, just slightly, as she sits there on the lid of the toilet. She takes another sip from her mug, then she says, 'I know. I do try, Felicity. Honestly. But he's all snappy – on edge. Oh – I don't know. It'll come right. We've just reached a . . . what's that word – a watershed. We need to look at where we're going together, what we want – stuff like that.'

Underneath my vanilla bubbles, I'm half relieved, half *cringing*. She's talking like a teenager, the way I talk to Simon. What does she mean – where we're going together? She's *here*, isn't she, she and Dad? Why can't they just be here, like they've always been?

'You know – it's different now the three of you are older,' she's saying. 'There's time to take stock of things – take in a big deep breath and think about what *I* want for a change. When you've got young children you just get on with it. You're too tired to think about yourself. You just do what you have to do to get through the day and keep everyone OK and keep the money coming in. And it's *hard*. You know, back then, when you were all small, we both worked as hard as we could. We really did. Dad was plugging away at his job, and away travelling a lot, and I was holding the fort at home. D'you remember moving?'

'I remember moving here. It was awful.'

Mum smiles sadly again. 'I know – you took ages to get

used to your new school. I remember just crying with relief, the first time you brought a new friend home for tea. Anyway. That was the *third* move we'd made, Fliss, since you were a tiny baby.'

'I know,' I mutter. 'I know it was. I've seen the photos.'

'It's bloody hard work, uprooting yourself, fixing up a place, signing on with a new doctor, finding out about playgroups and schools, making new friends...'

'So why didn't you say you didn't want to go?'

She shrugs. 'I didn't feel I had much choice. Dad got these great new job offers, and they meant moving, and that was that. And in a funny way it was OK, it was what I wanted. And we were in it together, you know? It was like – we were on the way up, with a bigger house each time, more money... I don't know. We were probably far too focused on the future. On how it was going to be. But at least we were both looking in the same direction.'

I make myself say: 'Were you happier then?'

Mum's staring at the bathroom wall, not seeing it. 'I don't know. I don't think we thought about it. Dad would get really down, all overworked and stressed out, and I'd buck him up, look after him, tell him things'll get easier soon. You know, I was giving him a neck massage one night and I remember thinking – Are you doing this because you love him or because he's the wage earner and you've got to get him back on track?'

'And which was it?'

'Don't know. Both, if I'm honest. You see – we *had* to keep at it. There was no room for manoeuvre. If I got flu, I couldn't just stay in bed, I had to get up and look after you lot. No family nearby to help, no close friends – it takes time to make close friends. I'd get really down too.

I felt I was suffocating under all the drudgery – loading the washing machine, grilling fish fingers, wiping people's bums . . . well, only your three bums.' She sniffs out a little laugh at me, but I can't join in. The water in the bath's getting cold and the stone's still there in my stomach. I'm glad we're talking at last but I'm scared too, scared of what she's going to say next.

'Dad could never see I had it as hard as him,' she goes on. 'I remember talking about how I was going stir-crazy at home and all he could say was "Stick it out till Phoebe goes to school," as if I could shelve what I was feeling until then.'

'Why didn't you get a childminder or something?'

'Neither of us wanted that. Look – don't get me wrong, Felicity – it wasn't all drudgery. I *loved* being with the three of you. I loved being there for the special times, making your birthday cakes and going out for picnics and everything . . . we had fun, didn't we?'

I nod, and Mum goes on, 'I wouldn't've had it any other way. It's just . . . you know. Sometimes you need a change.'

There's a silence, and I'm thinking about saying the water's getting cold and I want to get out of the bath, when Mum sighs and says, 'The thing is, my idea of change seems like going back, to him. Back to the days when he got back to a house that looked like a bomb-site and me all exhausted. He just doesn't get the point – that I *need* to do this. You know what he said to me the other night? I told him I might try to get hold of a cleaner, just to give the place a good going over once a week, and he said – "But you're earning less than a cleaner does now." So I gritted my teeth and said, "But

I won't be soon. Once I get the company up and running, I could be earning quite a bit." And d'you know what he said?'

'No,' I mutter, although I can guess.

'He said: "Well, as soon as you're earning as much as a cleaner, go ahead." Honestly, he's such a – it's all about *money*. He just won't support me.'

There's a silence. I'm really cold now but I can't move. Then Mum sort of shakes herself, and stands up, pulls a big towel off the radiator and hands it to me. 'Sorry,' she says. 'Sorry, Fliss. I shouldn't go on about all this to you. It's not your problem.'

Then she leaves the bathroom, shutting the door behind her, leaving me thinking – Not my problem? How stupid can you be?

Eight

I hold out until seven-fifteen that night, waiting for Simon to phone me, then I phone him. I get his mum. She says, 'He's not here, Felicity. He went round to Tom's to watch the match.'

'But that finished hours ago!' I blurt out.

'Och, you know what the lads are like when they get together. They've probably gone out for a burger or something.'

I take a deep breath, then I say, 'Do you have Tom's number?'

'Er – no,' she answers, and I know she's lying. She just doesn't want to give it to me. She thinks I'm way too possessive. 'I'll get him to ring you when he gets back, shall I?'

'Yes please,' I mutter.

I put the phone down, stalk off into the living room,

snatch the TV control away from Alexa, ignore her yelp of protest, start channel hopping like a lunatic.

Oh, *great*, Simon, I'm thinking. Spend all your money with your mates so you don't have any left to spend with me. Use up our Saturday night with your stupid friends while I sit here watching crap TV. And I can't stand your mum. The way she said you'd gone out for a burger. Like she was gloating.

I sit there staring at the screen, not watching, and I'm thinking – how can it ever work, with a man and a woman? Men suck. Monogamy sucks. Why isn't Simon more mature? I want a mature relationship, not some stupid kid who'd sooner go off with his goofy mates than spend time with me. I want him to want me, really *want* me, and not anybody else, not have room for anyone else.

What's happened to him? He used to be all over me when we first started going out together, he couldn't see enough of me. He used to say: 'I can't believe it. You're actually my girlfriend.' And he'd tell me about that time he just spent 'worshipping me from afar', never thinking I'd agree to go out with him.

Now we've got in this rut. This boring routine. It'd be different if we were sleeping together, wouldn't it? He wouldn't want to piss around watching football and going off to stupid burger bars then.

'Fliss? Hi. It's Simon.'

It's half past nine. He's waited till half past nine on a Saturday night to phone me.

'Hi,' I say, deadpan.

'Mum said you'd called.'

'Yeah. About three hours ago.'

'Oh – right. The match was ace, Fliss. I got there for most of the second half – we hammered them.'

'Great.'

'Look – sorry I didn't phone earlier.'

I'm silent.

'We went out for a pizza, then we got a few jars – you know.'

He sounds really pleased with himself, with his 'got a few jars'. I bet he had to hide in the background while Max went up to the bar. Stupid immature git. I stay silent, hating him.

'Look – don't go all mardy on me, Fliss. D'you want to go out now?'

'Now? It's a bit late, isn't it?'

'Yeah,' he breathes, all relieved. 'I reckon so. I'm knackered. All that sea air.'

I know what he's up to. He's reminding me of the big effort he made, of what he gave up, to go to the coast with me this morning. Suddenly, I just want to get off the phone. I don't want to mess around playing these mind games any more. 'Look, I gotta go,' I say. 'See you Monday, yeah?'

'Yeah,' he says, all conciliatory. 'See you, Fliss.'

I could've said I'd like to see him Sunday but he often has a big creepy family day then, with a fat roast and his uncles and aunts and close family friends and it's not worth the hassle to even ask if he can fit me in too.

I put the phone down without really saying goodbye, go up to my room, and put on *La Traviata*. I turn it up really loud. Then I lie on the bed all rigid and wait for it to happen, wait to get torn free from the shit state I'm in.

I've had this thing for opera since I was about twelve.

53

Especially women singers – divas. I love it when they open their mouths and soar. It's like they're going to crack open any minute with the force coming out of them, but they never do. And when I listen to them sing I literally shake with it, I think I'm going to crack with it too, I'm just going to split open and let it fill me.

I lie there listening. I know this opera now, I know what's coming. I start climbing and flying with the music, no room for anything else inside me, and it feels like it's fixing me, it's curing me. My mind floats free – the stone inside me disappears, I'm waiting to get torn open and washed up high . . . I listen, straining for every note. But there's something wrong. There's a grating, stabbing noise underneath the music, a noise that shouldn't be there. I try to ignore it, I try and follow the high flight, but I can't, it's ruined. I get up off the bed and turn the music down; then I go to the door and listen to what's happening in the hall.

'For Christ's sake, Stephanie – it's Saturday night! Don't you ever let up?'

'Look – I want to get it sorted out *now*. While you're here. Which is a rarity nowadays, isn't it?'

'Don't start about that again. It's not as though this place is any kind of pleasure to come home to, is it?'

'Oh, for God's sake – look. All I'm asking you to do is get back from your precious job two hours early on Tuesday so you can pick up fish and chips and the girls won't be on their own all night –'

'And I'm telling you I can't. What about Felicity?'

'She does enough. She's always stepping in. And she's got lots of coursework to finish off at the moment . . . it's not fair on her. That's why I'm asking you!'

'I've got too much on.'

'You've *always* got too much on!'

'That's right. That's how I bring home the salary I do. Look – this is your problem, not mine.'

'Oh, that's nice! So your kids aren't your problem.'

'Don't twist what I'm saying. If you think you can run a business, start doing it a bit more professionally. Organise some back-up.'

'Oh, that's rich. Only the other week you were laying into me because I wanted to find a cleaner –'

'I'm talking about babysitting.'

'Jesus CHRIST, Martin, they're your kids too! This was a last minute booking – I'm asking you to help me out –'

'You're not listening to me. I can't.'

'Don't adopt that snotty tone with me, Martin! *Christ*, you cold bastard. All those years I supported you, let you moan on endlessly about your job, spend half of Saturday in bed when I'd've given anything to have a break from the kids –'

'Oh, for *God's* sake, Stephanie, shut up. I made the money, you took care of the house and the kids. That was the deal. I don't remember you complaining about my pay cheque every month.'

'You sicken me, you know that? It's all money, money, money.'

'Try living without it, *Stephanie*.'

He says her name like he loathes the feel of it in his mouth. I back away across the room, turn my music off, get into bed still in all my clothes and jam my head under the duvet. I don't want to hear any more.

It doesn't matter what they're saying. It doesn't matter who comes out on top in the row. They're never going to agree, never. They hate each other too much. It's there in everything they say, in their voices. They hate each other.

Nine

Monday break at school, Simon finds me. He hurries over to where I'm standing on the outskirts of Liz's group, who are all jabbering away about this party they went to at the weekend, and reaches out with one hand like he might be about to put an arm round me. Then he drops it and brings his other hand up with a bag of crisps in it and says, 'Want one?'

I take one, but I don't smile. He's clearly feeling guilty and I'm glad. I'm also so relieved to see him it scares me. He jerks his head away from Liz's group, and then we both kind of shuffle off together, and head down the grungy path beside the tennis courts. There's nowhere to sit, but at least it's a bit private.

'I've got an invitation for you,' he announces, looking all pleased with himself.

'Yeah? What?'

'Burns' Night.'

'What?'

'You know, that old Scottish poet. He's got his own night. It's next Friday, the twenty-fifth. Dad said we should have a real hoolie, seeing as no one has to get up early the next day.'

'You mean it's with your parents?'

'Yeah, Fliss, it's Burns' Night. Mum cooks up this haggis and mashed tatties and neeps –'

'What? Sounds disgusting.'

'It's just mashed swede and potato. It's OK. Haggis is OK too, once you're used to it. Uncle Andrew digs his kilt out, and reads out various bits of crap poetry, and everyone gets arseholed on whisky.'

'Sounds great,' I say, sarcastically.

'Well, it's actually quite funny. Seeing them all make tits of themselves. Anyway. I don't have a choice whether I go or not. It'd be like missing Christmas. They're making a party of it this year, and Mum said I could ask you along too.'

I scuff my foot along the ground. I feel like making trouble. 'I'd sooner have our normal Friday night,' I say. 'Seeing as we don't always get to see each other on a Saturday.'

'Oh, Fliss – don't go on about that! I said I was sorry! Look – I'll see you this Friday *and* this Saturday, OK?'

'God – don't force yourself!'

'I'm not! What are you so ratty about?'

'Nothing.'

'Come on, Fliss – cheer up.' He tries to put his arms round me, but I push him off. 'What's up?' he says.

'Oh, nothing,' I mutter, relenting. 'It's just – your

parents' Burns' Night doesn't exactly sound the most fun thing in the world.'

'Yeah, I know. But honestly – I'll get flayed alive if I don't go. Dad'll go on about me spurning my Scottish heritage. Honestly, it's not worth it.'

'God, Simon. D'you have to do everything they want?'

He gets that look on immediately, kind of hurt and defensive. He hates it when I hint that he's weak, not man enough to stand up for himself. 'I don't,' he says. 'No way. But it'd really hurt them if I missed this unless I had a really good excuse.'

'And I'm not a really good excuse?' I'm spoiling things, I'm spoiling the last few minutes we have together on our own, but I can't help it.

'Well . . . they've asked you to come, haven't they?'

The buzzer goes for the end of break. 'You gonna come?' he asks, as we start walking back.

'I'll think about it,' I mutter.

Wednesday night comes round and I'm half thinking I'll not bother going round to Simon's house. I don't know why, really. I just feel pissed off with him, like he's taking me too much for granted, like he should treat our relationship as more special. He hasn't said anything about it being our six-month anniversary soon. I can't believe he's forgotten. I don't know what I'll do if he forgets.

In the end, I do go round, of course. It's just so grim at home. *Home*. I don't even think of it as home now. Home should be your refuge, shouldn't it, home should be where you feel safe, home shouldn't make you feel sick inside.

Mum's got a big do booked for Friday night and she's

channelling all her frustration with Dad into working flat out for it, baking and freezing stuff like a lunatic. She's pulling Alexa and Phoebe in with her, letting them fill little pastry cups with savoury gunk so that they think they're helping, but she can't console me that way. I can't bear the waiting, anyway. Waiting for Dad to come back. Or the way Mum looks at her watch, phones his mobile, leaves a really acid message because he's not picking up...

'So how are you, Flissy?' asks Simon. It's so good to feel his arms round me I forget about feeling pissed off with him. I push myself closer and pull his head down to mine, kiss him like I'm starving for him.

'Blimey,' he says, pulling back and smirking. 'What's got into you?'

'I missed you,' I say. 'I miss never having any time with you.'

That horrible, defensive, hunted look crosses his face and he says, 'Oh, come on, Fliss – we get time together!'

'Not enough. And it's never private. I mean – here, we're waiting for your mum to burst in. Or we're at the cinema, or just wandering about, or...'

He stops me, kisses me again. 'Wouldn't you like to just go away together, Si?' I breathe.

'What – like on holiday?'

'Yeah, maybe. Just go. So we can be alone.'

'Um – yeah. Sure I would.'

'Why don't we then?'

'Where?'

'We could go somewhere for the weekend. Somewhere cheap. Youth hostelling, even.'

'What do we tell our parents?'

'We lie.'

He's stumped for words. The plan's unreal to him, he knows we won't do it. I want to be with someone who'd *do* it.

'OK,' he says. 'Let's think about that one.'

Then he fastens his mouth to mine again, and pretty soon his hands are moving down on to my chest, and then we're side by side on the bed doing through-clothes petting. We daren't undo any buttons or zips on account of his mum being liable to rush in at any minute. He tries to wriggle his hand down the front of my jeans but they're too tight and his hand gets stuck in the waistband and he has to really pull to get it out again.

'It's *hopeless* here,' I moan. 'Wouldn't it be great to be away somewhere we could just be – totally free?'

Simon brings his head up sharp and looks at me. 'D'you mean what I think you mean?'

I can't get my eyes up higher than his left shoulder. 'Yes,' I say. 'Don't you want to?'

'*Yes!* God – yes! Course I do, Fliss! *God!*'

His words boost me, fill me full of good feeling. He wants me, he really does, he must do. I lay my head on his shoulder and we sit there on the bed, side by side.

We don't mention sleeping together again that evening. Not that we've exactly discussed it, we just both know we've agreed. We spend the time listening to music, chatting, holding hands, and it's like there's something new and special there now, this bond, this decision we've made. His mum raps on the door at about nine o'clock to ask us if we want a cup of tea, then she asks me if I'm coming to their stupid Burns' Night, and I say, 'Yes please, Mrs Addison. If that's all right.'

★

The next day Simon and I pass each other in a corridor in school, and we smile and walk on, not saying anything. It's like it's still there, the link, the understanding that we're going to sleep together. I feel all warm and pleased as I walk into the science room but then it's weird, this other feeling floods in, a sudden horrible feeling of sadness, or regret or something, and it comes into my head that I wish I felt more in love with him. I wish I felt like the heroine of *La Traviata*, singing. All starry-eyed and soaring and smitten, just thinking about him.

I shake it off though. I open my books and volunteer to help get the experiment equipment out and I'm thinking – No bloke's perfect, is he? Opera's for the stage. And those girls who go on about how in love they are, how wonderful their guys are – they're just immature, kidding themselves. Simon and me – our relationship's OK. It's real.

We go to the cinema on Friday night, just turn up without checking what's on first, but there's nothing much we want to see. I want to try for the 18 showing but Simon says he's not bothered. I know why, it's because he looks young for his age, and he's not sure he'll get in. They're always more careful about your age at the weekend and Simon's no good at bluffing it: he goes all red and looks younger than ever. It turns out there's only one film with space left that we can get into. We can't think of anything else to do, so we buy one carton of popcorn between us and find our seats halfway back.

It's really third-rate. I make myself concentrate on it, though. I don't want my mind wandering off onto other things. And then – as if the director knew how boring it was – there's this big drawn-out sex scene in the middle.

Nothing really pornographic, because it's just a 15 after all, but you know what's going on all right. I feel incredibly turned on and excruciatingly embarrassed both at the same time, and Simon goes all rigid at my side. I bet he's worrying about the smooth way the hero operates. I bet he's thinking he won't measure up.

Afterwards, we walk home slowly, and there's all these people weaving about in the town centre, loads of couples wrapped round each other, drunk and noisy, and this feeling of hard-edged partying going on. It seems to infect Simon. He pulls me over to one of the little roads that run off at right angles, and soon we're leaning up against the corner of Wallis, kissing. Then he's got his hand up my jumper and pretty soon it's moving round to the back, trying to unhook my bra. 'What the hell d'you think you're up to?' I hiss at him, half laughing.

'Come on,' he says, 'I thought you were the one who wanted to take it further . . .'

'Not on the bloody *high* street I don't.'

He drops his hands and looks at me. 'I think my folks might be going out tomorrow night,' he mutters.

Suddenly, I feel cornered. Suddenly, I feel cold.

'I want to go away,' I say. 'I want us just to . . . get out of here. I don't want it to be all rushed and . . . and on edge, in case your parents get back early or something . . .'

He looks sort of relieved. 'OK,' he says. 'But you could still come round, yeah?'

'Yeah. If you want.'

''Course I want. Or we could –'

'What?'

'Well – Max has started seeing this bird. She's *seventeen*.'

'So?'

63

'We could make up a foursome. Go out somewhere. You know.'

I hate it when he says that, I hate him wanting to be with more people than just me. 'I'd sooner not,' I say, starchily.

His face screws up. 'Why?'

'Cos I'd sooner it was just us two, that's why.'

He looks away, shrugs. 'God, Simon,' I explode. 'I thought you understood. You *know* what's been happening for me, you *know* what I've been going through...'

He looks straight back at me, all angry, and says, 'Look, Felicity, a lot of people have problems at home. You can't let it...'

'What? Can't let it what?'

'Oh, I don't know! You let it get you down so much!'

'If your parents were splitting up I'd like to see how happy you were!'

'You don't *know* they're splitting up, though, do you? And you're letting it really get to you, and... I dunno. It's daft.'

I won't speak to him after that, I just start walking towards the bus stop. He catches up with me and says 'Sorry', but I can tell he doesn't really mean it.

I get back home about eleven-thirty. Simon sees me to the end of my road like he always does. It's really quiet, at home, and all the lights are out except the hall one. I feel dead uneasy, but I tell myself it's OK.

I tell myself it's nice and peaceful for once.

Ten

Looking back, I knew something big had happened the minute I walked through the front door Friday night. As I walked up the stairs, even the air felt different: clotted, ominous. But I shook the thought off and rolled myself up in my duvet like a pupa switching off for the long cold winter and fell asleep.

Mum wakes me Saturday morning, shaking me gently but insistently, saying my name over and over again. 'What is it?' I groan. 'What time is it?'

'Ten o'clock.'

'Ten o'clock! It's Saturday, Mum.'

'I know, I know. Look – Dad's here. He's just got here.'

'What? Where was he last night then?'

'Can you get dressed, darling? Just throw something on, and come downstairs.'

I feel sick when she says that, so sick I think I actually am going to throw up, because I know it's happened, what I've dreaded has happened, but my mind won't connect, not even enough to ask her what's going on. I pull on some tracksuit bottoms and an old sweatshirt, then I go into the bathroom and clean my teeth but don't wash my face.

When I get downstairs, everyone's in the kitchen. The girls are finishing off bowls of cereal, looking straight ahead of them with huge, empty-looking eyes. Mum's pouring boiling water from the kettle into the teapot. And Dad's just standing there, leaning against the wall, arms folded, still with his jacket on, looking down at the floor.

It's surreal. It's fake. No one's saying anything. But I can't say anything either.

Mum carries the tea over to the table and pours out three mugs, one for me, one for Dad, one for her. Then she turns to Phoebe and Alexa, draws her lips back over her teeth in a smile that no way connects with her eyes and says, 'Shall we go swimming today?'

The girls look confused, scared, like someone's trying to trick them. 'When?' asks Alexa.

'Well – I thought after you've finished breakfast. We can have a really long time in the pool and then we can have lunch at the swimming pool café.'

Phoebe brightens. Lunch at the swimming pool café means chips and she loves chips. 'Is Daddy coming?' she pipes up.

'No,' says Mum. 'I'll take you.'

'And then tomorrow – I'll take you somewhere,' says Dad. He clears his throat. 'What about the cinema?'

No one answers. The girls are looking from him to Mum and back again. I think about saying something, asking what's going on, why I have to be down here listening to arrangements to go swimming, but I can't speak.

'Why can't Daddy come swimming?' Alexa asks.

'I've got things to do here,' says Dad.

Even from across the room, I can hear or maybe just feel Mum breathing fast and tense like she wants to start screaming. She's holding her mug of tea with one hand and the other one's resting on the table, only it's not resting, it's clenched, clenched in a fist. She looks up at me as if she's begging for help. Then she blurts out: 'What's happening is, Daddy's going to be moving out for a while. So while we're swimming, he'll be packing a few of his clothes together.'

'What?' wail Phoebe and Alexa together.

'Where's he going?'

'*Why* is he?'

'Oh, Phoebe. You know we had a fight last night, don't you?'

'Yes,' says Phoebe.

'A big fight.'

'Yes. You woke us up.'

'I know,' croaks Mum. 'I'm sorry, darling.'

'And we called out for you, but you couldn't hear cos you were shouting.'

'I know, I know. It was very bad of us, it was wrong. It made us realise we can't carry on like this because it's just not fair to you.'

There's a silence. Mum looks over at me again, that same desperate pleading look, but I can't make my face move, I can't do anything other than just stare blankly back. Then Phoebe whispers, 'Why d'you have to *fight*?' and starts grizzling and her nose starts running and she puts up a hand and wipes it across her face.

Mum's on her feet in an instant, round the table to Phoebe, who reaches out both arms to her like a baby. She kind of topples sideways and Mum catches her and then Alexa's off her chair too and all three of them are in this untidy, grieving, hugging mound on the floor.

I can't stand it. I look down, and the air round me feels like it's all being sucked away, and I can hardly breathe, and once I've looked down I can't look up again.

I know Dad's standing there, he hasn't moved, he's still leaning against the wall. I think if he so much as unfolded his arms it would shift everything, change everything, but he doesn't, he's frozen.

'It's just – look, Phoebe,' Mum's crooning, 'you know sometimes with Helen – you're best friends most of the time, then sometimes you just have to get away from her?'

I hear Phoebe gulp, whisper, 'Yes.'

'Well Daddy and I feel a bit like that now. We're so . . . *cross* with each other, we've got to get away from each other for a bit. That's all. We're fed up with fighting, we *hate* upsetting you when we fight.'

'And when you're not cross with each other any more, Daddy'll come home?'

That's Alexa. Her voice is thin and high with the strain of not crying. Moving just my eyes in their sockets, my eyelids feeling like they're weighted with lead, I look up.

I watch Mum torn between wanting to be honest and wanting to make everything less horrible. 'We both still love you girls as much as ever,' she says, pleadingly. 'Nothing will ever change that.'

68

'But when'll he come *home*?'

'He'll see you lots. He'll take you to the cinema tomorrow, if you want.'

Then Dad clears his throat again and says, 'What would you like to see?'

Nobody says anything. Does he really expect them to come out with a list?

'Let's get our swimming things, shall we?' asks Mum, with desperate brightness. And she shoots a look full of hate over at Dad, and grinds out: 'Sort some towels out for us will you?'

Dad peels himself off the wall and slopes out of the door. I risk a glance at his retreating back. It looks wretched, defeated. I'd like to bury an axe in it.

'Come on,' Mum's saying, in this horrible cheery voice. 'Let's get your cozzies, then. And where's your float, Alexa? You can practise leg kicks again, you're getting really good at them aren't you...' She prattles on while she shepherds the girls towards the door after Dad. And then I'm left in the kitchen all alone.

I can't move but my mind's racing, screaming. Why do we have to do this? Pretend it's not happening? Jolly the girls along as though a bag of chips and a cold chlorine dip'll take their minds off what's really going on? Why can't we be honest about how awful it is, why can't we all just collapse together, cry together, talk about it, talk about how scared we are instead of letting the fear set like cement inside us?

'Felicity?' Mum's poked her head round the door. 'Why don't you come too, darling?'

I shake my head furiously.

'I don't want to leave you here on your own...we can

have a chat, just the two of us, while the girls are in that play area by the café…'

I shake my head again, mutter, 'I've got loads of work to do.'

There's a pause. Then Phoebe, from the top of the stairs, shouts 'Mum!' She sounds as if she's about to start crying again. Mum shuts her eyes, like she can't take any more, then whispers, 'You sure you'll be all right, Fliss?' and I nod and she disappears.

I wait while I hear the three of them clatter downstairs, and Alexa calls out in a trembly, falsely bright voice, 'See you tomorrow Daddy!' And Dad calls down something I don't hear and I don't suppose Alexa does either and then the front door slams.

I make myself move. I cross the room and fill the kettle. I'm thinking – I'll make another mug of tea, and put three sugars in it, and then I'll phone Simon. I'll say I want to see him right away. He won't refuse, not when I tell him what's happened, he can't.

I get this weird feeling flowing into me then, almost of pleasure. It's happened, I think. At last, it's happened. I told you so, Simon. I told you things were this bad, and you wouldn't believe me. And now you owe me. No matter how upset I get, you can't blame me for it. You've got to look after me now, you've got to, or what sort of bastard would you be?

The kettle boils and clicks off and I make myself a mug of tea. Then just as I'm spooning in the sugar I hear this big bump on the ceiling right above me. I recognise the sound – it's the second-largest suitcase being pulled down from the top of the wardrobe in Mum and Dad's bedroom. I stir the sugar, round and round. I can hear

Dad walking to and fro in the bedroom above, I can hear drawers being opened and closed. I lift the sickly tea to my mouth, take a sip, take another. I hear the wardrobe door being banged shut, then the bedroom door. Then I hear Dad coming down the stairs with the heavy case shunted along beside him.

He's reached the hall. I hear the sound of his car keys being picked up from the hall table. I'm waiting for him to come into the kitchen, I'm dreading him coming in, I want him to just go, get out of here, I've got nothing to say to him, what do you say to someone who's walking out on you?

I take another sip of scalding tea, waiting, then I hear the front door slam.

Eleven

As soon as I can move, I go into the front room and dial Simon's number. After every ring I pray please, please let him answer. After five rings, his mum picks up the phone.

'Can . . . can I speak to Simon please?' I stammer.

'Well, he's trying to finish off some art work at the moment, Felicity,' she snaps out. 'He's got two bits of coursework to hand in and the deadline is Monday. He's only just got down to it.'

She's expecting me to say 'Oh, OK then, sorry' and ring off. I don't though. I take a deep breath and say, 'I just have to speak to him quickly. I need to tell him something.'

She hesitates – huffs impatiently, the cow – so I grit out, 'I'll be really quick.' She dumps down the receiver. I hear her calling 'Si-mon' irritably up the stairs, then nagging at him as he comes down.

He picks up the receiver and says, 'Hi.'

'I've got to be quick,' I say bitterly. 'Your *mum* says so.'

'She just —'

'Dad's left home.'

'Oh, Christ.'

'You know you kept saying I didn't have to worry about my parents splitting up till they announced it? Well they have.'

And then I start crying. And I don't move the receiver away, I just cry straight into it.

'Oh, Fliss. Oh, God. Look — I'll come round. I'll come now.'

'No!' I wail. 'I don't want to stay here. I need to get away from here.'

'Sure. Look — what about The Mulberry Bush?'

'I can't go to a café! Not like this!'

'OK. Come here.'

'Will you make sure you open the door to me?'

'I promise. I'll wait in the hall.'

Half an hour later, we're sitting side by side on his bed, and I'm telling him the whole horrible story, especially the way I felt totally alone, with Mum only concerned about Alexa and Phoebe, and Dad walking out without saying goodbye.

'Maybe your dad really thought you'd gone swimming,' says Simon, all consoling.

'He could've checked. He could've just stuck his head round the kitchen door to check.'

'Yeah. But when you think about the state his head was *in* — I mean, he must've felt like shit, packing his case to move out. He must've felt really sick.'

'Too sick to find out what state I was in?'

'Yeah, well. You know.'

'The fact is, Simon, I didn't even cross his mind. He doesn't give a damn about me – he doesn't care. All he thinks about is himself.'

Simon puts his arms round me again and holds me, and I press my face into his shoulder and cry. 'I'm making your shirt wet,' I sniff.

'Doesn't matter,' he says, gently.

'Oh, Si, thank God I've got you. I love you. I don't care about them.'

'Yes you do. That's why you're hurting so bad.'

'Yeah, well, they're not going to hurt me any more. Long as I've got you, I don't give a shit what they do. They can die for all I care.'

'You don't mean that.'

'I do. I'm just going to eat and sleep there, and work for my GCSEs, and see you. Do you love me?'

'You know I do.'

'That's all I need. They're not going to get me.'

We sit there on the edge of the bed and Simon rocks me, and again I get that feeling that I wish I could die right now, while things are OK, while I feel loved.

Then there's a tap on the door and Simon's mum opens it before we even get a chance to answer. 'Max and Tom are downstairs,' she says softly. 'It's twelve-thirty.'

Simon looks stricken. He automatically checks his watch, then he says, 'Shit. I should've phoned them. Look – I'll come down. Tell them I'm just coming, would you Mum?'

She disappears without a word. 'Did you tell her?' I ask.

75

'Yes,' Simon says. 'D'you mind?'

I shake my head. I know the only reason he told her was to get her off our backs. 'So what were you doing?' I ask. 'With Tom and Max?'

'Going bowling.' There's a pause, then he says, 'I'll go and tell them it's off.'

I hang on to his arm as he tries to stand up. 'Can't your mum tell them?'

'Well –'

'You said you'd told her what'd happened.'

'Yes I know, but I said I'll be down in a minute to see them.'

I let my hands slither off his arm and he stands up to go. At the door he turns round and looks at me pleadingly. 'I'll only be a minute Fliss, OK?'

I don't answer. I let my face say – even a minute's too long.

I spend about four hours at Simon's house, just shut in his bedroom with him. At one point he goes down to the kitchen to make some sandwiches – I tell him I'm not hungry but he says I need to eat. While he's downstairs I stand in the open door of his bedroom and try to hear what his mum's saying to him. It sounds like she's just asking him questions. There's a pause after each of them and then Simon answers. He sounds tired, weary. No matter how hard I strain my ears, I can't hear what they're actually saying. But she has to back off now, doesn't she? She has to accept that Simon really needs to be here for me now.

As I leave to go home, I make Simon promise to phone at seven, so we can decide if we want to go out or not.

He says he'll do whatever I want to do, but that I'll probably just want to go to bed and sleep. 'And drink, Felicity!' he says as he's kissing me goodbye. 'All that crying – you'll be dehydrated!'

I try to laugh at that, because I know he wants me to. He means it, too. He thinks of that kind of thing.

I get back home about five o'clock. The usual Saturday teatime sounds hit me as I let myself in the front door – cartoons from the back room, clatter from the kitchen. I stand there in the hall for a minute or so, thinking I'd like to just slip upstairs and get under my covers and sleep until Simon phones. But Mum sticks her head round the kitchen door.

'Fliss! Where've you been? Have you been to Simon's?'

I nod, and she goes on, 'You might've left me a note, darling. I mean – I guessed where you were, but –'

'You could've phoned Simon's house,' I say, deadpan. 'If you were really worried.'

Mum's face kind of contracts in on itself, then she says, 'Look – come and chat for a minute. I'm just finishing off some onion tarts for Tuesday night.'

She disappears into the kitchen again and I drag myself in after her, because it takes less effort than saying 'No, I want to go to bed now.' The table's covered with crusty, toffee-coloured tarts, the air is thick with onion smell. 'I'm going to have to get a bigger freezer,' Mum says. 'I thought I could put it at the back of the garage. Things like this – they freeze really well.' Then she smiles at me, as though she actually expects me to be interested, points to a tart with a big burnt bit on the side, and says, 'That one's a bit of a failure. We can have it for tea. With a bit of salad.'

'I'm not really hungry,' I say.

There's a pause. Mum pulls another tart out of the oven, and says, 'I'm really sorry about just – landing that on you. This morning.' She puts the tart down on the table, shifting some of the others aside to make room for it. Then I think she stands and looks at me but I can't be sure because I keep staring at the tarts.

'Thanks for being so understanding, darling. You know. With the girls and everything.'

Understanding? I wasn't understanding. I just didn't say anything. 'Why d'you have to tell us all together?' I blurt out.

'Well – I – I don't know. I didn't know how it would go . . . I thought you might all be a support for each other. And . . . and . . . oh, *look*, Felicity, I just had to get it *over* with! I couldn't stand the thought of going through all this more than once.'

'When did he decide?' I mutter. 'To go?'

'Well – last weekend, we talked about it. Dad's got a friend he can stay with, near work. It's just – it's been getting impossible. We had another row, last night . . . and he . . . *well*. He walked out.'

I look up at her, finally, and I can see her eyes filling with tears, but I don't feel anything for her. 'You said you were working it out,' I croak. 'You said this bad time was just a watershed.'

I remembered the word because I had such a strong picture of it in my head. In my picture, even though I knew she'd meant it to be positive, water was filling this low dark shed, climbing higher and higher, drowning everyone inside.

'Well – I hope it is,' Mum whispers. 'I hope . . . after

we've had a break from each other... I hope we can take a new direction, work things out.' Then she turns away, back to the oven, and it's like she's suddenly really angry, and she spits out, 'Look — I didn't chuck him out. He wanted to go. He said he couldn't take one more row. Then, first thing this morning — eight o'clock it must've been — he phoned and said he wanted to come and get his stuff.'

'What did you say?'

'Not much.'

'You could've asked him not to.'

'Why the hell should I? He'd made his decision — to walk out on me. *Us.* And frankly, Felicity, part of me was relieved! Just to call a stop to it all, to get some space here, not to feel churned up with all that anger and tension all the time... We're going to have a real break from each other. Time out. Then we'll see.'

There's a long pause. She heads over to the fridge, pulls out lettuce, tomatoes, and says, 'You sure you're not hungry?'

I shake my head. I can't speak.

'You know,' she says, gently, 'it's not all bad. It's going to be more sorted out — more businesslike, almost. He's suddenly all eager to see lots of you girls, for a start. Taking Alexa and Phoebe to the cinema tomorrow. When did he last do anything like that — at least without a big row first?'

So that's all right then, I think sarcastically, as I trudge upstairs. The family's sorted. Mum's going to buy a big freezer and Dad's going to take the girls to the movies and everything's sorted. Great.

I don't put my opera on because I feel numb and I

want to go on feeling numb. This great tiredness has come over me, a great swamping, blanking-out tiredness, and I give in to it gladly. I slither under the covers and fall asleep.

When I wake up it's really dark. I reach out and pick up my bedside clock and peer at it – it's seven, on the dot, which is when Simon said he'd phone. I must be getting telepathic or something. I wait, counting each breath, and at breath number twelve the phone starts ringing downstairs. My whole body kind of sighs with relief, relaxing. Then I lie back, close my eyes, and wait, listening to Mum climbing the stairs, opening my bedroom door quietly.

'Fliss?' she calls softly. 'Are you awake?'

'Tell him I'm asleep,' I whisper. 'Tell him I'm tired out.'

Twelve

On Sunday, Mum is determined it's going to be business as usual. You have to admire her determination. She sees the girls off to the pictures with Dad at midday, and sets about making a big roast for Sunday lunch, which we eat at about four in the afternoon. This is a good halfway time, Mum says. Time to have a morning first and an evening afterwards. Dad always hated eating then, said it was neither one thing nor the other. Eat at lunchtime, he used to say, or wait until it's dinnertime. Now we can eat at four with no arguments.

And when Monday comes round Mum makes the packed lunches first thing as usual and we all go off to school as usual and in a way everything's as usual and nothing's different. It's just like Dad's gone off to work early or something. And in the evening, it's like he's away on a business trip. Except it isn't the same, because Mum's trying too hard to be cheerful and capable, and the girls are still trying hard not to cry, and there's a kind of space behind everything we do, a gap we don't know how to fill, a big unsureness about everything, about why we're all here together, and I catch Alexa watching Mum, just watching her, as if she's afraid she might leave home too.

At about half-eight, Liz phones. She's all choked up and teary – she's heard on the grapevine about Dad walking out. 'Why didn't you *tell* me?' she keeps saying. 'I can't believe you didn't tell me.'

I mutter a bit about not wanting to talk about it yet because I'm feeling numb and stuff. She tells me of course that's how I feel, she understands totally, but please will I phone her or grab her the minute I want to share how I feel. 'I hope you know I'm always here for you, Fliss,' she says. '*Always*.' Her voice is all quivery and shaky and I feel miles away from her because right now I can hardly feel a thing. I mumble on again about just wanting to block it all out at the moment, hoping that'll get her to leave me alone. She says she understands and she's going to buy me a big bar of chocolate to cheer me up and she'll bring it into school tomorrow. Something in my head knows how kind she's being, but I don't feel it.

Not long after that, Simon phones, asking if I'm OK. I tell him – not really. We don't say much. What matters is that he's phoned.

That night in bed I get this thought, as strong as if someone's said it straight into my ear: I'm here on this earth because those two loved each other. Now that's all over, where does that leave me?

★

On Wednesday night there's another change. Mum's catering partner Jan pitches up with a whole carload of utensils and provisions, and carries them into the kitchen. She's come to cook side by side with Mum, preparing stuff to freeze for an engagement party on Saturday. Our kitchen's bigger than hers, Jan says, and her house still has a man in it. I can hear them joking about it as they chop up vegetables together. 'Ach, I envy you,' Jan says. 'All this space to yourself. Freedom to do what you want in it.'

Mum laughs, and Jan says, 'I *do*! I envy you. D'you know – sometimes I feel so stale.'

'Well,' Mum says, 'stale's the last thing I feel right now. I'm on some kind of a high. A bit hysterical, but still high. Like I've been kick-started.'

'It's the adrenalin. From all the drama. And the relief – you know, from finally doing it, going over the edge.'

'You make me sound like a soldier.'

'You are, girl,' Jan says, and they laugh again, loudly. I shoot upstairs, partly in case they catch me eaves-dropping, partly because I don't want to hear any more.

The week passes. Simon, Liz, Megan – they're all saying kind things to me, but it's like I'm underwater or something and I don't really hear them. That feeling of numbness I had on the day Dad walked out is still there underneath everything else. And I'm *tired*. I sleep loads, and when I sleep, I dream. I dream about being small again, and Dad carrying me, picking me up and hugging me when I'm hurt, when I'm frightened. I feel his arms round me, his strength; I smell his cotton shirt and the aftershave he uses, and I wake with a sense of loss so horrible I can't move, I can't move until the feeling in the dream fades and I tell myself it was a long time ago that he was like that, and I tell myself to get up and get on with reality.

When I'm not asleep I'm listening to opera – nothing else. All my other CDs sound weak and shallow and fake-happy or false-sad next to opera. I play *Don Giovanni* over and over again, especially the bit at the end where the stone statue comes for Don Giovanni and takes him off to hell. It scares me, the deep, deep way he sings – the way there's no escape, this is it, over – but it thrills me too, it frees me, and I can't stop listening to it.

We don't see Dad at all that week. On Thursday night, I know Mum speaks to him on the phone, and I know it's bitter and angry and about money. She screeches, 'But why d'you need to take out that much? We'll be overdrawn!' She cries afterwards, up in what used to be their room. It's a furious and pathetic sound, and I think about going in to her, but I don't, I can't, I can't even offer her a cup of tea through the closed door.

Friday comes round. Burns' Night and the 'hoolie' Simon asked me to, what seems like a whole lifetime ago. 'You're still coming, aren't you?' he asks me, catching up with me after school.

'Oh, God, I don't know. I haven't thought about it.'

'No, 'course you haven't. Look, Fliss – come. It'll do you good. Make you forget about everything.'

'Well . . . Dad's supposed to be coming round tonight to take us out to eat, or something.' And I think of me, Alexa and Phoebe, lined up opposite Dad in some pizza parlour, trying to chat.

'Well, it's up to you, Fliss.'

'Yeah, it is. Yeah, Si – I'll be there.'

★

84

I turn up at Simon's doorstep at ten to eight that night but it's not Simon who opens the door to me. It's some fat, bearded guy I've never seen before, wearing an enormous kilt and a stupid tartan hat with fake red hair hanging down, who I think must be one of Simon's uncles. 'Who's this?' he roars, jovially. 'She looks *English*!'

It's meant to be a joke but it isn't and I don't laugh, although I smile a bit in self-defence.

'Andrew, don't you start,' says Simon's mum, appearing beside him. 'This is Simon's girlfriend. Ignore him, Felicity. Scotsmen who've moved to England – they're always the worst. The most nationalistic.'

'Aye, well, we need to be!' Andrew booms. 'Surrounded by sassenachs! Come in, lass! Joyce – where's the lad?'

'He's upstairs, trying on that kilt you've forced on him.'

'*Forced* on him?' roars Andrew, all mock-indignant. 'It's his heritage – he should be proud and eager to wear it!'

'Yeah, but not when it's about a million sizes too big,' says Simon's voice from the top of the stairs.

Everyone looks up, and Simon's mum calls out, 'Come down, then! Let's admire you!' and Simon starts swaggering down the stairs, all into the joke, with this massive kilt bunched round him with a big wide belt.

'Thing is, Uncle Andrew,' he says, 'just cos it's far too small for you now, doesn't mean it's gonna fit anyone else – anyone who isn't about ten stone overweight that is!'

Andrew bellows like a bull, rushes up towards Simon and grabs him. He gets him in a headlock, and Simon flails out with his arms and slithers free, laughing, and Simon's mum's all 'Boys, boys, stop it now before one of you gets hurt!'

I can feel myself closing down inside. Right down. All this jolly family stuff – it's sick-making. Simon glances across at me and says, 'What d'you reckon, Fliss?' He hasn't even bothered to say hello to me. He grins and pulls out the sides of the kilt like a little girl in a party frock.

'Great,' I say, flatly, and look away.

'You see?' says Andrew. 'Felicity thinks it's great. You have to keep it on, Simon, nephew of mine. Or I'll strike you out of my will, so I will. Now – we just have to find some tartan for wee Felicity here.'

What? I have this sudden hideous vision of being forced into the female equivalent of what's wrapped round Simon, and squeak, 'I'm fine. Honestly.'

'Assuredly you're fine. But you need some tartan. It's Burns' Night!'

'Simon didn't tell me,' I say. It comes out all starchily. I don't really mean it to, but it does.

'I despair of you, lad!' groans Andrew. 'Not telling the lass she needed to wear tartan on Burns' Night.'

'I don't have any, anyway,' I mutter.

I can feel Simon's mum looking at me. 'Simon, take Felicity through and get her a drink,' she says.

As I follow Simon down the hall, the doorbell goes again, and there's more noisy hubbub as Andrew greets the next guests. 'Sorry,' smirks Simon, 'he's totally mad.'

'Are you keeping that stupid kilt on?' I hiss. Simon looks down and mumbles something I can't hear, and ushers me into the back room. His dad's in there, with about six other people, all kind of screeching at each other like they want to prove they're having a whale of a time already. Normally Simon's dad's a real in-the-background type, but tonight he's handing round beer and whisky and he's gone very loud. 'Hello, kids!' he cries. 'Simon – you look ridiculous!'

'He looks terrific!' comes from another part of the room.

Simon's dad grins broadly at me. 'What'll you have to drink?'

My mind goes blank. What am I s'posed to say? Is alcohol allowed or what? 'I'm fine,' I croak out, idiotically.

'Have a beer,' says Simon, rescuing me. 'We'll both have a beer, Dad.'

Simon's dad's just poured them out when Andrew bursts through the door, booms 'Those for me, Dougie?' and picks up both glasses.

'Oi, Uncle Andrew, those are for us!' says Simon, all joke-furious.

'You're too young to drink!'

'I am *not*!'

'Aye you are!' Andrew takes a huge pull from the glass in his right hand, then one from the left. I can feel my face setting hard. He thinks he's so funny, such a laugh – well, I don't. He's a pig. A rude pig.

Simon glances at me, laughing, trying to get me to laugh too. I know he's torn between wanting to please his family and not wanting to piss me off, but I don't help him out, not one bit. Simon's dad meanwhile has poured out another couple of lagers, and he pushes them into our hands, then he announces to the whole room that I'm Felicity-Simon's-girlfriend. I back away, heading for a corner. Simon follows me. Then this woman calls out in a real snotty trying-to-be-funny voice, 'What I want to know is, how come I had to put these ghastly plaid trousers on, while Felicity gets to wear that lovely dress!'

'It's not plaid,' roars Andrew, 'it's tartan! D'ye know nothing, woman?'

She throws her head back and laughs. 'Plaid, tartan, it's all the same to me. I was told I had to wear it on pain of death!'

'You do,' says Andrew. 'Felicity's going to wear ma bonnet, aren't you, lass?'

There's a general roar – Simon laughs too, looking at me, willing me to join in. It's all a big joke I'm not in on. I feel frozen.

'She can't wear that hideous thing,' says another woman, crossing over towards me. 'Here, Felicity. Take my scarf.' And she pulls this stupid woolly tartan scarf off her neck, and winds it round mine.

I don't want it. I hate having it touch me. I want to chuck it off on the floor.

'Thanks, Auntie Jean,' says Simon. And then his mum sticks her head round the door and calls out, 'All right, everybody – take your seats! We're ready to dine!' and Uncle Andrew starts on about how there should be a piper and makes these horrible bagpipe noises down his nose. We all troop out of the back room and into the big kitchen-diner. I pull at one end of the woolly scarf and it drops to the floor. Simon pretends not to notice. My heart's thudding and I feel something like panic. I'm thinking – I can't go through with this. I can't sit there for hours on end while everyone acts the fool and pretend I'm having a good time. I grip Simon's hand tight and he squeezes back as though he thinks I'm just being affectionate.

Simon's mum shepherds us into seats together at the end of the table. It's been moved to the centre of the room and it's got all its extensions pulled out with chairs from all over the house crammed round it. His mum's made a real effort – candles, plaid paper napkins. I feel a bit better once I'm sitting down, leaning against Simon. His dad makes a big deal about seating everyone else. 'Come on – boy, girl – boy, girl!' he chants.

Uncle Andrew's mouthing off, making a fuss about reading 'the verse'. 'Who's got the book?' he keeps trumpeting. 'Dougie – where's the book?'

Simon hands me a dish with dip in the middle and these posh-looking crisps round the outside. 'How long's this going to last?' I hiss. He shrugs, eyes pleading, then he tips the rest of his beer into my empty glass.

The noise level round the table rises up and up, as everyone hands the starters round and Simon's dad pours more drinks. I finish my beer, get a refill, eat some of the crisps but not the dip – it smells disgusting, like rancid fish. I try to talk to Simon but people keep interrupting, calling out jokes, trying to involve us in their stupid chat.

Simon's mum gets up and bangs around at the cooker for a few minutes, then she calls out, 'OK – it's ready!' and carries a big tureen of yellowy-looking mash over to the table. Andrew jumps to his feet looking self-important, clutching a little leather-bound book. Then a big plate with two steaming brown humps on it appears, and Andrew does his stupid bagpipe noise again. He picks up a big sharp knife in one hand, shouts 'To the haggis!' and starts to read from the book. I don't understand a single word he says but it sounds really revolting. He's hamming it up like anything, roaring and making disgusting guttural noises. Everyone but me is just about falling over with hilarity, cheering and banging on the table and shouting 'aye'. Then he pauses melodramatically, waves the knife, says something about 'gushing entrails bright', and cuts into the haggis. 'Dammit, Joyce, this isn't sheep's stomach, this is plastic!' he bellows, and everyone shrieks with laughter as he carries on ranting from the book.

It's like everyone's gone mad. And my panic's come back, worse than ever. There's something horrible and vile coiled up inside me – it's growing, and the pressure's unbearable.

I sneak a desperate sideways look at Simon – he's fixated on his uncle, nodding and sniggering, mouth hanging open like an idiot. 'I can't eat that,' I hiss.

'It's OK,' he hisses back. 'It's tasty.'

Andrew has started splatting bits of haggis onto plates, and Simon's dad adds a splat of yellow mash, then the plates get passed clockwise round the table. It looks about as appetising as the worst school dinner ever made. The man to my right passes a plate to me, but before I can land it on to Simon, Andrew shouts out, 'Hang on to that one, lass! I dinna want it back again!' And I sit and look at it steaming nastily in front of me, trying not to breathe in the musky smell, thinking I can't bear to put any of it in my mouth.

Soon, everybody's served. 'Well, y'failed on the casing!' Andrew's going. 'Plastic indeed! I hope it's good sheep's innards inside and not some namby-pamby blend of mincemeat!'

'*What* did he say?' I hiss at Simon. '*Sheep's innards?*'

'None of your carping, Andrew,' says Simon's mum. 'This is the best haggis money can buy!'

'*Sheep's innards?*' I repeat.

'Oh, Fliss – just try some,' snaps Simon, and turns to

say something to the woman next to him. I sit back in my chair, stung.

'Come on, start eating!' cries Simon's mum. 'Don't let it get cold!' And everyone starts chowing down. I don't even pick up my knife and fork. A large bottle of whisky is making its way slowly round the table: some people are pouring it over their haggis; some people are pouring it into their glass; others are doing both. The whisky reaches Simon, who splashes a little on his plate, then tips a bit into his empty beer glass. He tries to hand it to me but I won't take it. Then just as he's pushing it past me Andrew swoops down like a fat vulture and picks it up.

'Try it, lass!' he says. 'Try just a bit on your haggis.'

I shake my head furiously. 'No thanks.'

He leans over the table. Close up he's even more disgusting. Grease is streaked down his beard, like snail tracks. 'Come on, just a splash,' he says, and tips the bottle forward. Whisky gushes onto my plate, and before I can think I'm snapping out, '*I said no!*'

I say it louder than I mean to. People nearby stop talking, turn to look at me.

'Oh, Andrew...' Simon's mum begins.

'Well, she wasn't touching it plain!' Andrew goes, spreading out the hand without the whisky bottle in it, all innocent. 'She hadn't had one mouthful!'

The whole table's looking at me now, I know it. The smell of the whisky hits me, mixing with the rank smell of the haggis. I stand up, push my chair back noisily. 'What's up, Fliss?' hisses Simon.

'I...I think I'm gonna be sick,' I mutter.

Thirteen

I make it out to the hall. I'm not going to be sick, but I've got to get away from everyone, I've got to. I grab hold of the handle on the front door and twist it and I'm off down the path, leaving the door open. I can hear Simon shouting 'Fliss! Fliss – wait!' but I don't wait, I keep on running, and then when I get to the end of the road I slow down a bit and he catches up with me.

He's carrying my coat – he's panting. 'What's wrong?' he cries. 'Why d'you run out like that?'

I want him to put his arms round me but he doesn't, his face is all cold and confused and angry. 'I shouldn't've come,' I mutter. 'It was a mistake to come.'

'Why, for heaven's sake? It's just a party...'

'Look Simon – don't shout at me please! I feel like shit – I feel awful! I just couldn't stay one more minute in there. OK?'

'I don't understand –'

'*Look* – just take it from me I couldn't. You could've stayed. You didn't have to come after me.'

He's silent, breathing heavily, glaring down at the ground.

'Why don't you go back,' I spit out, 'you don't have to miss it.'

'Come back in with me.'

I feel like I want to smash him in the face when he says that, I hate him, I hate him for not understanding.

'Come on,' he goes. 'We can say you just felt ill for a bit and now you're OK.'

'I'm *not* OK,' I hiss, 'and there's no way I'm going back in there.'

'Fliss –'

'*No!*'

There's a long pause, then he says, wearily, 'OK, then. I'll see you back home, all right?'

'Don't bother. You go back. You don't want to miss it.'

'Oh, it'll be half over by now. Anyway, I don't want to face all their questions, do I?'

'What questions?' I ask, bridling.

'Oh, what was wrong with you – why you dashed off like that without even saying goodbye to my mum or anyone –'

'*God*, Simon, all you care about is the fact that I might have offended your mother, isn't it. I shouldn't've come.'

'Oh, stop saying that.'

'*Look* – I'm sorry I messed up, OK? I feel really screwed up and shitty and I'm just going to go home and go to bed. OK?'

He looks down at the ground again, and when he

looks up again his face looks softer, more resigned. 'It's hitting you really bad, isn't it?' he mutters.

'Yeah it's hitting me bad. How d'you think you'd feel if your dad suddenly walked out?'

He puts his arm round me. 'Come on,' he says. 'I'll see you home.'

As we walk back to my place, the awfulness of what I did, just storming out like that, hits me, and I think: I can't ever phone his house again. I don't care, though. I've gone way past caring about stuff like that. When we say goodnight I make him promise to phone tomorrow, at seven on the dot. We kiss, but it's a bit weird, a bit half-hearted, like he's kissing an invalid or something. 'When d'you think we can go away together?' I whisper. 'God – I want to go away with you so much. Just the two of us.'

'Yeah . . .' he murmurs.

'Well, when?'

'Easter maybe?'

'Oh, God – why do we have to wait that long? Why can't we just go? It's all unreal, Simon. Home's unreal – my family – everything's unreal apart from you.'

'Oh, Fliss.'

'I love you, Simon. D'you love me?'

'Yeah. Yeah, Fliss, you know I do.'

We fight on the phone, the next day at seven on the dot. Simon wants us to go along to The Hedgehog and Stump and meet up with his mates. He says it'll 'cheer me up'. I can't believe he's that stupid, that insensitive. I don't want to be in some big crowd. I say I just want to see him, and in the end I get my way and we go to a grim, plastic pub on the far side of town where they never bother to ask how old you are before serving you.

It's not a good evening. I ask him if his mum said anything about me running out of the party, and he just shrugs and looks all evasive, and says he told her I wasn't feeling well.

'Your Uncle Andrew was enough to make anyone feel ill,' I say.

'Oh, he's OK,' Simon mumbles. 'He's just a bit over the top sometimes but –'

'A *bit*? He chucked about half a bottle of whisky over my plate! And he kept making all these nasty comments –'

'Oh, Fliss – they weren't nasty! He was just trying to get you to loosen up a bit and join in!'

'So you're on his side now, are you?'

'Don't be ridiculous, it's not about sides –'

'You thought I was all uptight too, did you?'

Simon shifts about angrily on his seat, then he says, 'I just thought you'd've had more fun if you'd joined in a bit. I mean – you didn't even taste the haggis.'

'I'd sooner put dogshit in my mouth.'

'Yeah, and that was written all over your face!'

'I can't help that.'

'Well – it pissed people off, that's all.'

'Oh, we're getting to it now, are we? What was your mum saying?'

'Just – like I said. How you didn't join in.'

'I didn't want to! I thought they were all pathetic!'

There's a long silence. Simon picks up his beer and takes a drink. I want him to agree with me, I want him to say what a horrible evening it was, but he won't. We end up talking about stupid things, like how awful the barman's haircut is.

I feel really depressed when I go to bed, really hopeless. I wish Simon was more...I wish he didn't disappoint me so often. All Sunday, I'm just dragging about. I shut myself in my room and tell Mum I'm working on an essay and she believes me because that's what she wants to believe because it means I'm out of her way and she can concentrate on having a lovely family time with the girls downstairs. They're doing dough-modelling today. Phoebe shows me all excited as I go down for a mug of tea. 'Look Fliss – it's a doggy! I'm going to bake it in a minute!'

Alone in my room, I don't do much work. I just sit and feel lousy, buried. I tell myself everything'll be different once I get away with Simon. He'll be different. I'll be different.

Fourteen

After what happened on Burns' Night, I'm nervous, going round to Simon's as usual on Wednesday night. But I don't want to miss it. Sitting side by side with him on his bed, talking, kissing, making plans – looking forward to that is just about the only thing that's kept me going since the weekend. And, I think, it's not like I'm going to have to see his parents or anything, is it? Simon promised me I wouldn't have to.

That's why it's such a shock when it's Simon's mum who opens the door to me.

I feel really humiliated, standing there face to face with her, no idea what to say, nothing prepared. I feel like I disappear deep inside myself. How could Simon let this happen?

Simon's mum breaks the silence. 'He's out,' she says abruptly, in this strangled voice. 'Look – come through a minute, will you?'

I don't even think of arguing. I follow her into the kitchen like a sheep. She turns and faces me across the kitchen table, looking like she's trying to make her mind up what to do. There's such a long silence that in the end I'm the one who breaks it, by croaking out, 'Where is he?'

She takes a breath and says, 'We had a row. He stormed out. It all started...over these.' Then she fishes in her pocket and drops a packet of Durex on the table, as though it's something vile, something pitiful.

I feel like she's slapped me. It dredges me up from where I'd disappeared to. My eyes are fixed on the shiny packet.

'I found them in his top drawer,' she goes on.

'You went through his drawer?' I blurt out.

She bridles. '*No*. No, Felicity, I did not go through his drawer. I was putting some clean socks in his drawer like I do every week and there were these...condoms. Clearly visible. Not even in a bag. Now, I'm not a qualified psychiatrist but I'd say that maybe sub-consciously he *wanted* me to see them, wouldn't you?'

I shrug and keep glaring at the packet on the table. I can't seem to shift my eyes from it. And I'm not giving her the satisfaction of looking at her, no way. 'Maybe he wanted you to know he's not a kid any more,' I mutter.

'Not a kid –? He's still fifteen. And he's young for his age. Too young for all this, anyway.'

'So that's what you had the row about.'

'Yes. Well – put it this way, it was the beginning of it. We started off talking. Once he'd got over the shock of me producing those damn things, he wanted to talk.'

I look up at her, stung. 'I can't believe he discussed... *that* with you.'

100

'Well he did. And I'm glad he did. He's all confused about it – about you and him – he's *upset*. I just don't think he's ready, Felicity. For that kind of relationship.'

I let my lip curl. 'Don't you think that's up to him and me?'

'Yes, I do. But that's the point. He thinks it's not up to him. He thinks you're . . . he says you're pressuring him.'

My face floods with colour. 'He said that?'

'Look – he's not one of those lads whose main aim in life is to jump into bed with the first girl who'll let him. He thinks about – you know – the consequences. And I'm actually . . . I'm proud of him for that. He knows if he starts sleeping with you . . . *well*. It's too big an involvement, Felicity. You're too young, and the way things are . . . it's all wrong!'

I glare at her. My cheeks are still burning.

'God, I don't know if I should be saying this to you,' she rushes on. 'I don't know if I'm doing more harm than good. But I can't just stand by and watch him being made so unhappy, I can't. All this strain you're under, what you're going through with your parents and everything – it's putting *him* under an enormous strain, too. And I just feel . . . *well*. You want to jump into a big adult relationship with him because everything's gone so wrong for you at home.'

'That's not the reason,' I mutter. 'I love him. We love each other.'

'Maybe you do. But you're getting so intense! You're both too young for it to be this intense, and now you're talking about sleeping together . . . I know why you're doing it, Felicity. You're hanging on tight to him because everything else feels like it's crumbling away.'

I'm silent, glowering at her, and she goes on, 'You know – I've got enormous sympathy for you. Don't look at me like that – I have. But Simon can't solve all this for you. He can't heal everything for you, all the hurt. He's just a kid.'

'I don't expect him to heal everything for me. How can he?'

'You say that, but he feels responsible. He feels like he's all you've got – all you want, sometimes. It's too much to lay on anyone, Felicity.'

I can feel my face burning again, burning like anything. Simon must have told her the things we talked about, repeated what I said to him when I was feeling really, really close. I feel so betrayed I can't speak. And then I remember something.

'Why did he storm out?' I ask, coldly. 'What did you say to him?'

She drops her eyes, clears her throat. She rubs at a mark on the table with her finger.

And in a flash I know. She was telling him to finish with me, that's what she was doing.

Fifteen

I don't say anything else, I just turn around and walk out. I don't care about Simon's mum and what she was saying, but I'm furious with Simon, furious that he's been such a pathetic limp inadequate, furious that he's been talking about *us* to his mother. I jump on a bus at the end of the road and sit at the top, just boiling with rage, looking out for him as the bus rocks along. All I want to do is get face to face with him and tell him exactly what I think of him.

I get off the bus at the end of our road, go straight up to my room and put *Tosca* on very loud, right at the end where she's full of anger and rejection and hate. I'm soaring along to her voice, flat on my bed, eyes shut, and suddenly someone's patting my leg, hard. My eyes snap open and there's Simon standing beside me.

'How did you get in?' I gasp.

'Alexa.'

'I didn't hear anything!'

'I'm not surprised, with that racket on.' And he marches over and turns it off, bang, just like that. 'Look, Fliss – we gotta talk.'

'You bet we gotta talk. You *idiot*. Leaving a packet of condoms out where your mum could find them, and then telling her just about everything – I mean, *Christ*, what sort of a pathetic idiot are you, Simon, having to have a chat with your mum about sleeping with your girlfriend? If you think I'm gonna come anywhere *near* you after this you can think again – you're *pathetic*, Simon, really pathetic.'

I don't know what I'm expecting. Him to shout back, or plead, or something. Not this, though. Not him just standing and looking at me, like he's seeing me for the first time. He's got one hand gripped in the other so tight it's turning white.

'I'm sorry that happened,' he says at last, flatly. 'I'm sorry Mum was there when you got round. I was in such a state I forgot you were coming round.'

'Oh, *nice*. She really laid into me.'

'No she didn't. She told me what happened.'

'Oh great! So you ran back to Mummy again, did you, before you came here?'

'I went home cos I remembered you were coming round. Mum told me you'd just left, she said what'd happened. So I came out to find you.'

'Big of you.'

'Fliss, can you *stop* this? This – spiky, spiteful shit? We've got to talk.'

I shrug, furiously. 'Go ahead then. You immature idiot.'

He shoots me a look full of hate then, and says, 'OK.

OK, maybe I am too immature. Maybe I'm too young and immature to get involved like you want.'

My stomach seizes with fear. Something's shifted.

In the room, everything's shifted.

I wish we could stop, rewind, go back to where I open my eyes and see him standing there, and this time I won't be so vicious, this time I'll see his side of things, this time –

'We want different things, don't we,' he's saying. 'You want this full-blown relationship, you want someone who's always there for you, never lets you down, doesn't want anything else going on in his life . . .'

'That's not true,' I interrupt.

'It *is* true! It's just – it's getting so heavy.'

'But that's only been since Dad walked out –'

'No it isn't! Since Christmas, since before Christmas – everything's changed, Fliss. Between us. Look, I couldn't believe my luck when you first said you'd go out with me. It was so great, at first. I was full of it – I'd really piss my mates off, going on about you all the time. And we had a brilliant time, didn't we, we really talked . . . just being with you made me feel good. And when you started to talk about the shit that was happening between your mum and dad – well, I felt really glad you could – you know, open up to me.'

There's a pause. Why's he doing this – summing up what our relationship was like? Like a flashback of your life before you die.

'But it . . . I dunno,' he mumbles on. 'It's like it all started closing in. Like you expected so much of me, and it's like this big burden, now. My mates – they keep going on about how I'm practically married to you.'

'Is that all you care about? What your mates think?'

'No! No – I'm just saying – other people have noticed. That it's all got so heavy. And it's not good any more, is it? You're unhappy all the time and we fight and –'

'Look – I know I've been a pain,' I croak. My throat's gone so tight I can hardly speak. 'Bad tempered and stuff...' My whole face is pleading with him but he can't see it. He's not looking at me, he's looking at the floor.

'It's not just that,' he mutters. 'You're hanging on to me so tight it's – it's strangling me, Fliss! It's suffocating!'

'Well – I'm sorry. But – *God*. It's been horrible recently, if you can't –'

'Look, I know how bad it's been. I do. I know what you're going through at the moment. You need someone to be there for you, support you and stuff. But – God, Fliss – you're putting it *all* on me and I can't – I just can't *carry* you any more. You want me to listen to you all the time and prop you up and ditch my friends for you and... and I'm going along with it but I don't really know why any more, I don't know why I'm doing it any more.'

I can feel everything in me collapsing. I want to clutch at him, scream, but I don't. I push it all down, stuff it down, make my face go stony. 'What are you trying to say?' I ask coldly.

'Look – I'm not criticising you. It's just – you need someone else, not me. Half the time I feel it's not me you want anyway. We just – we don't have fun any more. *Do* we? It's all got so heavy, and whatever I do, however I try to cheer you up, it's never good enough, and you always end up looking at me just like that, and – *Jesus*. I've had it. I've had enough.'

There's a long, long silence. I feel like I've been gutted,

literally, like all my insides have been dragged out of me. 'So you don't love me any more?' I whisper, at last.

'I – I – oh, *God*, I don't know. I don't know what I feel. I'm so weighed down it's like I don't feel anything. It's just – it's not working any more. Is it?'

'Are you saying we're finished?' I don't know how I get the words out. There's still this hope in me that he'll deny it, talk about how we can fix things between us.

But he doesn't. He looks straight at me and the relief on his face is somehow worse than all the stuff he's been saying. 'Yeah, Fliss. I mean – we can still be friends and stuff, we can –'

'Oh, *God* –'

'Look, Fliss, I'm not doing you any good like this and . . . I can't take any more. I'm sorry.'

It's like a door's slammed in my face. And all I can think of then is how to hit out at him. Make him share the hurt I'm feeling. 'So you did what Mummy told you to do after all,' I sneer. 'She told me you'd walked out when she said you ought to dump me.'

Simon looks dumbfounded. 'She never said that!'

'Why did you walk out then?'

'She said – stuff like I was doing more harm than good. Stuff like you needed help. You know. Professional help.'

It's like I can't breathe then, like I'm drowning. I pull my duvet up tighter round my face. 'You'd better go,' I say. 'Go on, just *go*.'

'I'll phone you. I'll phone you in a week or so, see how you –'

'Don't bother! Look – just go will you!'

He goes. And I pull the duvet right over my head and don't move, I don't move for hours.

Sixteen

I use hate to get me through the next two days. It's like I don't feel anything but hate: it's my energy. If I was a witch, I'd melt down wax and I'd make one model of Simon and another of his cow of a mother and I'd jab them full of pins – in their eyes, in their mouths, in their hearts, everywhere. As it is, I tell as many people as I can at school that Simon got scared because he knew I wanted to have sex with him, and I see people looking at him and sniggering, and I see him looking wretched and white and miserable, and it makes the hate burn better.

Friday lunchtime, Mac, one of the hardest guys in our year, bumps into me as I'm coming out of the canteen. 'I hear you didn't get no satisfaction, Felicity,' he says, all mocking, and his mate Joe laughs.

I shrug, embarrassed. 'What's it to you?'

'I could've told you not to waste your time on Simon Addison.'

'Yeah, well. I know that now, don't I. I should never've gone out with him in the first place.'

'So why did you?'

I shrug again. 'Look – it's history. Why are we talking about it?'

'Just – you could always come to me, darlin'.'

I laugh, all defensive. 'Oh, yeah? I'm not just after a stud.'

'Hear that, Joe? Fliss thinks I'm a stud.'

'I didn't say that! I'm not just after someone to screw, is what I meant.'

I walk away. He calls out after me, 'Well, think about it, Felicity! The offer still stands!'

I walk on and I can't help it, I feel flattered. Mac might be a thug with no brain but he's good-looking. He gets loads of girls. As I head into class for the next lesson I find myself replaying the way Mac looked at me. For the last few months Simon's looked at me like he's got to protect himself. Mac's look was nothing like that. Simon might not want me, but he did.

To Liz and Meg, I make out I'm not really that upset about Simon. 'At least I don't have to get him a six-month present now,' I say. 'When you think about it, we split up just in time.'

Liz laughs. 'I'm just amazed it lasted as long as it did.'

'Yeah. He was so young. I mean – he was really sweet but it was getting very boring. Very samey.'

They're looking at me like they're not sure they believe me. 'You must feel a *bit* sad, don't you?' asks Meg.

'Aaah – not really. It was time for it to end. I mean – he was just too immature to handle the next stage.'

They both giggle a bit at that, and Meg says, 'Don't you mind people talking about it?'

'Why should I? It's his problem.'

'H'm.'

'Why should I feel embarrassed? There're enough guys out there who'd sleep with me if they had the chance.'

'Well . . . sure.'

'In fact I had an offer only this morning.'

'Yeah?' shrieks Meg. 'Who?'

'Mac.'

They both groan at that, and Liz says, 'Well, I think it's great, the way you're dealing with it. But don't expect to just – you know – shut the door on it straight away, though, will you Fliss? I mean – especially now your dad's –'

'I'm fine,' I say, cutting her off.

'Yeah. Yeah, I know. But you're gonna get weepy days. You used to say how lovely it was having someone that gone on you . . .'

'Yeah, but it got too cloying, you know? It got stifling. It suffocated me.' I realise I've used the word Simon used to me, and I don't know whether I want to laugh or cry. I keep a straight face for Liz and Meg, though. Acting like it's all OK helps me believe it, helps it be OK.

'Club Nitrate,' says Meg. 'Tomorrow night.'

'You bet,' I rap back.

'They've got that really hot new DJ there – wossisname.'

'I know him!'

'Shut up Fliss – you know. Sokka D.'

'Great.'

'And Kaos.'

'Brilliant.'

'Meet up at mine about eight, yeah?' says Liz. 'We can get ready together. I've got some tequila in.'

'Great. I'll bring the lemon – Meg can bring the salt.'

And so I get through Friday. I'm coping, I'm fine. Mum's not home when I get back from school and Alexa and Phoebe are out, too. It's a relief, having the house to myself. I haven't told Mum about Simon dumping me yet. I'm waiting for the weekend, when I can be sure I can tell her calmly, sure I can deal with all her questions, sure I can tell her it's all under control.

I veg out in front of the telly for a while. There's nothing on. I end up watching this docu on the work girls did in factories in the 1950s before they got married. 'Light repetitive work' they called it – testing light bulbs, packing biscuits, filling perfume bottles. It looks quite nice, somehow. Kind of safely braindead. No aspirations. No chance of failure.

At five-thirty, Mary, our fat nosy neighbour from next door but one, arrives on the doorstep with the girls. 'Is your mum back yet?' she asks, peering past me down the hall.

'No.'

'Oh – I thought she would be. She said she wasn't going to be long. She just asked me to fetch the girls from school and hang on to them for an hour or so but they were having such a nice time with my Karen's old doll's house, I let them stay on for a bit longer and –'

'Thanks, Mary,' I interrupt. I want to get rid of her.

'She wouldn't tell me what it was about. Didn't she leave you a note?'

'I didn't find one.'

112

'I got the impression something had come up all of a sudden . . . oh well, I expect she's sorted it out. The girls've not had their tea, love. Just a couple of biscuits.'

'I'll get them something,' I say, and slowly, I start to close the door. Mary takes the hint, says goodbye, and waddles off down the path.

I turn to Phoebe and Alexa. Usually they'd head straight for the TV, but they're still standing in the hall, looking unhappy. 'Why don't you watch telly for a bit?' I ask.

'I'm hungry,' announces Phoebe plaintively.

'Where did Mum go?' asks Alexa anxiously. 'She didn't tell us Mary would be picking us up from school, and she always tells us if someone else is picking us up . . .'

'Oh, Alexa, don't fuss!' I snap. Out of the blue, I'm hit by the fear she's full of, and it unnerves me. She's scared Mum's going to walk out on us too, like Dad did. What happens to kids if both parents walk out on them?

'I'm not fussing,' whines Alexa, 'just –'

'You know what we're going to do?' I say, loudly. 'Order pizza!'

'*Pizza!*' crows Phoebe.

'Have you got enough money?' asks Alexa.

'Yup, I do. Now – you like the Hawaiian, don't you? With ham and pineapple?'

They both nod greedily, and trot off to the back room, and I hear the television start up. Then I go into the kitchen and look around for a note from Mum. Usually, if she leaves a note, it's propped on the stairs, but maybe if she was in a rush . . . There's nothing in the kitchen, either. I can feel these little fingerings of panic, working in my chest. It's just not like her to be back late and not tell us where she is. I think – I'm not up to this, I can't deal with it. Not now Simon's dumped me. I can't.

I shake that thought off, bat it away, and find Mum's emergency jam jar of money, put out of reach on one of the high shelves. It's got two ten-pound notes, a five, and a handful of pound coins. I take it all, and head for the phone in the hall.

While I'm dialling the pizza place, my eyes fall on Dad's mobile number, pinned to the red noticeboard behind the phone. If Mum's not back by seven, I think, or she hasn't phoned by then – I'll ring him. He might've left but he's still our dad isn't he?

The pizzas arrive, a large Hawaiian for them, a small pepperoni for me. We eat them with our fingers out of the boxes in front of the telly, the girls fighting over who gets the last slice. I don't want to look at my watch. I know it's nearly seven, and I feel weird about phoning Dad. He's out of Mum's life now – why should he know where she is? Maybe I'll wait till half-seven.

Alexa's got her arms round her knees and she's rocking herself, which is what she always does when she's worried. I want to snap at her to cut it out, but I stop myself. Then the adverts come on, and she turns to me and whines, 'Fliss, when d'you think Mum'll be back?'

I don't answer. I get up and walk out into the hall, pick up the phone and punch in Dad's number. It connects; it rings. And rings. I find myself thinking about why he's not answering: what he's doing. Then I get his recorded message. I listen to it to the end, but after the beep goes I can't think of anything sensible to say. So I hang up again. He'll know I called, though, won't he? It'll come up as a missed call.

114

I go into the kitchen and put the kettle on then, mainly because I don't want to face Alexa's huge worried eyes again, and then the phone goes. I rush for it, pick it up expecting Dad, but it's Mum on the other end, in a call box.

At least I think it's her. She sounds so different.

'Felicity? Look – it's OK. I'm OK. I'm on my way back. I'll be another couple of hours or so.'

'Where've you been? Why didn't you –'

'I'll tell you when I get back, OK? Would you do something for me? Would you tell the girls I'm fine and . . . and I went out with Jan or something – and would you put them to bed? Only I can't face them tonight.'

'What? Mum, you're scaring me!'

'It's OK, Felicity. I'm fine. We're fine. I'm just – look, I'll be back in a couple of hours, OK?'

And then she hangs up. I can't believe she just hangs up.

Seventeen

I do everything she asks. I manage to smile as I go back
into the living room and I spin out some lie about Mum
having a surprise night out with Jan whose sister is over
from Ireland, and they were having such fun she forgot
the time, isn't it *good* she's having fun. I even manage to
get the girls up to bed a bit early, I'm all jolly and I run
their bath for them and read them a story, and then I go
downstairs to the kitchen to wait.

Mum gets back, finally, at ten past ten. 'Are they
asleep?' she rasps out.

I nod. Her voice is still strange, like every word costs
her. I want to put my arms round her but I can't. I feel
almost afraid of her. I feel like I used to when I was little
and I'd want to hug her to stop her being angry but I was
scared to in case it made her worse. She looks dreadful –
white, ill – and she's so angry, she's crackling with anger,

and something else, something like hate.

'What's happened?' I whisper.

She walks across to the sink, fills a glass with water. Then she drinks it, and for a minute I think she's going to be sick, she's all bent forward like she's going to throw up into the sink. Then she puts the glass down and runs her wet hands through her hair, and turns round to face me. 'I'll tell you,' she mutters, her eyes lasering at me. Her hair's all on end where she's raked her hands through it, it's like snakes writhing, like Medusa.

'Your dad's living with another woman,' she hisses.

She's Medusa and if I look at her I'll turn to stone.

'*What?*'

'A girlfriend. He's moved in with a fucking *girlfriend*.'

I am stone. And her face is rigid, a mad, frozen mask. Her mouth's barely moving but these awful words are coming out, pouring out of her like acid. 'That lying bastard – oh, I can't bear it. I can't believe it. It's so . . . *hackneyed*. All those times he spent "working late at the office". It didn't occur to me to question it. And all those stupid rows we had, about me starting up my company and him not helping out enough – that wasn't the bloody point, was it? The point was he had someone else and he felt guilty about it so he picked fights and acted like a shit – I know what he was up to. He was trying to prove our marriage was over so it'd be OK to leave. All those rows, the way he was so bloody touchy, the way he stormed off and slept on the sofa every time we fell out –' She gags then, turns back to the sink, cranes over it, brings up some of the water.

My brain's numb. I can't fix on what she's saying. 'Oh, Mum,' I mutter. 'Mum.'

'I phoned him,' she grates out. 'At work. He'd had his mobile switched off, I'd left two messages and he'd not got back to me, and I needed to talk about money, all the money going out of our account...' She trails off then and gives this horrible laugh, and says, 'Well, at least I've cleared that mystery up now, haven't I? He was spending the money on her.'

She turns back to the sink, fills her glass again, then says, 'I got Harry instead – you know – the man he shares an office with? Harry and I always got on OK. He told me when your dad'd be back, and then he obviously thought he ought to say something because he sort of choked out, "Stephanie, I want you to know that in my opinion Martin's behaving like a complete idiot, and if there's anything I can do..." Well, I thought that was weird. The more I thought about it, the more weird I thought it was. And I just – I flipped. I knew I had to find out what was going on. Well – I suppose deep down I knew what was going on.'

'You mean you knew he had a girlfriend?' I croak.

'Kind of. It all fell into place, after Harry said that. All the working late, excuses that weren't quite right – that kind of thing. So I got Mary to pick up the kids, and I drove to your dad's office. I didn't know what I was doing, I just knew I needed to follow it through. I drove into his car park, and parked out of sight, watching his car. I sat there for hours. Then he came out. He had this woman with him. Nothing special – brown hair in a bob, quite tall. Younger than him. *Of course*. Could've just been a colleague. I wasn't sure. He was talking, and she was looking at him all the time, and they both got in his car. Then he drove off and I followed him.'

Mum's voice has gone dry and hoarse. She takes another mouthful of water; it looks like it hurts her to swallow. 'Wouldn't he have seen your car?' I asked. 'Behind him?'

'I wasn't that close. And they were pretty wrapped up in what they were talking about. He drove over to the other side of town where there're all these new flats. Really smart new developments. I parked across the road and watched him turn in. And then I watched them both get out of the car and ... he put his arm round her and she looked up and he kissed her ... He really kissed her.'

I still feel like stone. I'm hearing what she says, but it's not getting through, deep down it's not getting through.

'I wrote the address down,' she says, wearily, chucking a bit of paper on the kitchen table. 'I didn't wait around to get the flat number.'

There's a long, long silence. The only lights on in the kitchen are the little strips under the cupboards and usually it's cosy like that but tonight it just feels dark.

'You don't know he's living there,' I whisper.

'No, I don't. But it's pretty obvious, Felicity. He was all evasive about this "friend" he was staying with – wouldn't give me the phone number of the flat, saying he didn't want to impose more than he had to, told me to use the mobile ... And after they'd kissed, this woman went round to the boot of the car, and got out a couple of bags of groceries, and he took one off her as they walked inside. All very domestic.' She pauses, adds bitterly: 'He never helped me like that.'

'What did you do after that?' I breathe. 'Up until now?'

'God knows. I drove about. Went into a pub, had a double Scotch. I tried to phone Jan. I phoned you. I

120

parked somewhere, and just walked. I'm sorry I didn't get back earlier, but I felt so bad, I couldn't cope with it, and I didn't want you girls to see me like this –'

'It's OK,' I break in. 'It's OK. D'you want a cup of tea?'

'No, love. I'm going to bed. Look – thanks for seeing to the girls. I'll think of something to tell them tomorrow, some way of dealing with it. I couldn't hide it from you, though.' She looks up at me, wanting me to agree with her, reassure her she should've told me, and I manage to nod, like I understand.

'Don't say anything to them, will you,' she goes on. 'Tomorrow morning. Look – it'll be OK. He's left, we've split – why we've split doesn't really matter, does it? And I'll get over all the lies. Maybe it'll make it easier now, to make a new start.'

'But weren't you... I mean, you spoke about getting back together...'

'That's all it was, speaking. It wasn't really going to happen. You knew that, didn't you?'

I shrug. I hadn't let myself know it.

'I've got to get to bed now, OK, Felicity?' She totters over to the cupboard where she keeps the booze, and pours herself a glass of brandy. Then she goes out of the room, calling back, 'Turn out the lights when you come up, won't you, love?'

And I'm left there, bitter and frozen with everything she's told me. Dad's betrayed us. He's dumped us. Mum, me, Alexa, Phoebe – even all together we don't add up to the tall woman with the brown bob. The desperate thought comes in my head to phone Simon, tell him what's happened. He'd have to see me, wouldn't he. He owes me that much. I want to be with him when I start to thaw, when I start to feel things again...I can't, though, can I. I can't possibly phone him. I'm on my own now. I can feel this fear seeping into me, a terrible fear, fear of how I'm going to live from now on, with no one wanting me, and I slam down on it, hard, push it down deep inside me.

The scrap of paper Mum threw down is still lying on the kitchen table. I pick it up and read 'Magpie Place, Bridge Street'. Then I put it down exactly where it was before, so Mum won't know I've seen it, and I go up to bed too.

Eighteen

I wake up early, six-thirty or so. I think I can hear Mum crying in her room. I lie there, rigid. I can't move. All the phrases people use to make themselves shift – get up, get a cup of tea, get going – they won't work, they don't mean anything now.

Mum can't help me. She wants help from me. I can't help her. In my head I see Simon standing by my bed, saying, 'You're hanging on to me so tight it's *strangling* me, Fliss!' I see Dad kissing a stranger, taking a bag of groceries off her, going up to her flat with her.

They've done this to us, haven't they. It's their fault.

I must drift off to sleep again then because when I next come to it's nearly eleven o'clock and I can hear Phoebe chanting something downstairs at the top of her voice and I can hear Mum call out to her, all forced and strained and bright. I want to go to sleep again, just escape into deadness again, but I think – I can't, I've got to move, I've got to get going or I'll never move again.

So I pull on some jeans and an old fleece and slouch down the stairs. 'Hello darling!' says Mum. 'Want some toast?'

I look at her face; I can still see the mad mask from last night, somewhere under her smile, but only because I know to look for it. While I'm getting a plate out of the cupboard and the girls are occupied fighting over the scissors for the paper dolls they're making, she sidles up to me and whispers, 'I haven't said anything to them. You know.'

'So when will you?' I mutter back.

'Well – maybe I don't need to. What do you think?'

I shrug, and she goes on: 'He's coming at two today. He's taking them to Bales Farm for the afternoon. We fixed it up before . . . you know.'

'You found out.'

'Yes.'

'Mumm-ee,' calls out Phoebe, 'are there going to be pigs at the farm?'

'Yes, darling, you know there are. And goats and cows . . .'

' . . . and donkeys and horses . . .'

' . . . and ducks. And hens.'

'And will Daddy get us an ice cream?'

'It's too cold for ice cream, Phoebe. He's going to buy you your whole tea.'

Phoebe's so impressed by this she falls silent, and starts cutting out again, humming to herself. Mum hisses at me, 'I can't face him today. I mean – I'm going to have to face him soon. But not today, not with the girls here.'

I butter my toast, pour out a mug of tea, wonder if I'm supposed to be answering that, when she says, 'It'll be OK. They can let him in, can't they? I mean – we've organised the time, and when he's bringing them back . . . that'll be OK, won't it?'

'Yeah,' I mutter.

'It's just – if I even see his *face* right now, I'll go berserk, I know I will. I'll do something stupid. You know, all I can think of doing is getting in the car and going round to their little *love nest* and confronting him . . .'

I pick up my plate of toast and mug of tea, walk out of the kitchen, head up to my room again. I can't hear any more, I can't, I can't bear it. Mum scares me. It's like she's got something terrible inside her, waiting to burst out, and I feel I've got it too, growing inside me, sucking at my life . . . it wants to force its way out and I'm using all my will, all my energy, to keep it down.

I stay shut in my room, sat at my desk, looking down at my homework books, not doing anything. Mum shouts up at about two o'clock that she's made some sandwiches for lunch and I go down but I can only gag down half of one. Mum gives me a bright 'we're-coping-aren't-we?' smile, like we're conspirators, like we're plotting between us to keep Phoebe and Alexa safe from the truth. After lunch I go up to my room again and sit and do nothing. I hear Dad arrive. He rings the doorbell now, he doesn't just let himself in. I hear the girls fussing about, calling up to Mum, Mum calling down, all jolly and fake and off-you-go-then-girls, and I wonder if he's going to ask to see me and then I hear the front door slam behind the three of them.

I'm waiting then, on edge, wondering if Mum's going

to stick her head round my bedroom door, wanting to talk. I'm thinking what I can say to put her off. But instead I hear loud rock music start up in the kitchen. It plays for thirty seconds or so, then it gets louder. I put my opera on, and my headphones. I make myself follow every note of the music, so nothing else can get in my head.

Nineteen

That night, I set off for Liz's place about eight-thirty. On the way over I make up my mind not to talk to Liz and Meg about Dad and where he's living now. I'm sick of it, I'm sick of the whole thing, I just want to break out from all of it.

In my purse, I've got what's left of Mum's emergency fund after I ordered the pizzas last night. Around eighteen quid, plus some money of my own. I don't think about whether it's good or bad or dishonest or whatever, keeping this money, just that I'm flush. I march into an offy and ask for a bottle of tequila and because I've already made up my eyes and my voice comes out all hard and forceful, the guy behind the counter doesn't blink, just hands over the bottle.

I open it as soon as I get out of the shop, and take a long swig. It's rank, but I manage not to choke on it.

Fairly soon, I can feel it flowing sweetly into my bloodstream. I've hardly had any food today, so it's working fast. The vice in my head softens; the strangle-hold in my chest loosens its grip. I breathe better.

'Jesus, Fliss,' says Liz, as she opens her front door to me, 'I told you I'd got some tequila in!'

'Yeah, well, we can always save that till next time. I'm not paying for booze at Club Nitrate, it costs a fortune. Come on, let's set them up.'

I push past her, and race up the stairs to her room. Meg's already there, in front of the mirror, curling her hair with Liz's tongs. I wave the tequila bottle at her, and she laughs, 'You in a rush or something? Don't you want to wait till we're ready to go?'

'We can have another then,' I say. 'Come on.'

We started our little tequila slammer ritual nearly a year ago, because we liked the effects of alcohol but not the taste. We did it whenever the three of us went out together, like a kick-start to the evening.

Meg puts down the tongs, rummages in her bag, and pulls out a lemon. Then she picks up Liz's nail scissors and hacks it awkwardly into bits. Liz, meanwhile, is getting out the three tiny green glasses she keeps in her room. 'OK,' she giggles, filling them to the brim. 'Salt? Here – stick out your hand, Meg. Got the lemon ready? OK – Five! Four! Three! Two!' We lick the salt. '*One!*' We screech in mock-dread, and down the tequila, straight off, then we grab a bit of lemon each and suck it, to take the taste away.

'So – you been keeping this up, have you?' I demand. 'While I've been out of circulation?'

Meg glances across at Liz, and says, 'Not the same with

two. Anyway, we've been getting into white wine.'

Liz pulls a face. 'You've been getting into white wine. I think it's rank.'

'It's an acquired taste,' says Meg, grandly.

'Acquired taste? Aftertaste more like. Aftertaste of sick.'

While they're rapping at each other I pick up the tequila bottle and turn away, and before I screw the cap on I take one last swig. 'What time we aiming to get there?' I ask.

'Ten?' says Liz. 'Early enough to get in cheap, late enough for the place to've got going.'

An hour later, and we're all tarted up and ready to go, doing the tequila ritual again. This time I don't bother to hide it, I just tip myself out another glassful when I've swallowed the first one. 'Blimey, Fliss, watch out,' says Liz. 'You'll be falling over.'

'Yeah, I thought you looked wobbly when you put your heels on,' goes Meg.

'I'm *fi-ine*,' I say. 'Come on, let's go.'

'So,' says Liz, as we head for the bus stop, 'I s'pose you two are gonna be on some kind of rampage tonight. Taking revenge on the male sex and stuff.'

I look over at Meg. 'Why – what's happened?'

'Jake,' says Liz. 'He happened. Or rather his girlfriend did.'

'*What?*'

'He was seeing someone else,' Meg says, bitterly. 'I was right. She found out about me, and gave him an ultimatum and . . . he chose her.'

'Oh – nice!'

'What pisses me off is I respect her for it. I do. I mean

– I knew about her. More or less. But I didn't challenge him. She though – she wasn't swallowing any of that let's-be-free, don't-check-up-on-me crap, like I did.'

'Yeah, but you're better off,' says Liz, loyally. 'Now. I mean – she's the one who's ended up with him. Good luck to her.'

'I know. Stuff him. Stuff both of 'em!'

There's hardly any queue at Club Nitrate and we get in past the leering bouncer without any bother. I realise as I walk down the long dark staircase with its little side lights that I am pretty drunk. I'm kind of weaving all over the place. I don't care though. I feel OK. Better than I've felt for ages.

Sokka D is just starting up when we get down there. I've only heard him once before, and I've forgotten how great he is. He just moves into your head, takes over, commands you. Soon we're moving about, and the music's loud and pulsing, and I've forgotten everything, I'm just dancing, really wild, and shouting out to people, and there's this crush, and I lose sight of Meg and Liz, but it's OK, I just keep moving like it'll all crash down if I stop. Sokka D mentions me, he says, 'This is for the lady down there dancing like a dervish!' and grins at me. I dance on, really pleased he's noticed me. Meg appears at my side and gives me a bottle of water. I tip it into my mouth and half of it goes down my front and she squeals, '*Fliss!* I queued up for, like, *hours* to get you that!' and I laugh, and tell her it's lovely, having it splash down my front, it's all cool.

A bit later on, this guy who's been dancing near me for the last two records moves in and shouts in my ear, 'Want me to get you a proper drink?' And I say yes, and we

move off together to the bar. I ask for a tequila sunrise –
I reckon a bit of orange juice now will help with the
hangover later. It only takes him a few minutes to get it
because he's quite big and he leans over the other heads
and shouts to the barman. We stand up against the wall,
drinking our drinks. He's getting closer and closer to me
and then he takes the drink out of my hand and puts it
on a table and puts his arms round me and we start
necking, and I try to remember what he looks like but I
can't and it strikes me as dead funny to have your tongue
inside the mouth of someone you can't even remember
the face of, and I laugh.

He pulls back, says, 'What's funny?'

He's OK-looking. Bit rough-looking. Dark, broad-
shouldered.

'Nothing,' I gasp, trying not to laugh again. 'Nothing.'

'You want to dance some more?'

'Yup.'

He gets hold of my hand and we go back to the floor.
My energy's gone, though, and it feels like the walls are
wobbling about. I'm hardly dancing any more, just
swaying, and gradually, he's steering me across the floor,
steering me into a corner, and there's a little half-wall and
we're behind it and he's started kissing me again, and his
hand's on my breast and I jerk away but he pulls me back
to him and his hand's squeezing my breast so hard it hurts
and he won't stop jabbing his tongue in my mouth and
just as I think I'm going to throw up or something I hear
Liz's voice.

'Fliss? Fliss! Come on, girl, we gotta go. Cab waiting.'

The man stops, swears at her, and she swears straight
back, glaring at him. She puts her hand on my arm, tugs

me. And then the man goes all civilised and soft, like he knows Liz has won, and pulls a little, square, white card out of his pocket and sticks it down the front of my top. 'If you ever fancy a drink or something,' he says, 'give us a bell.'

'Oh – my – God,' Liz is going, as she tows me up the lighted stairs. '*Oh – my – GOD*. What an ego. There he is, mauling you like a dog with a dead rabbit, and then he has the nerve to dump his phone number on you. Let's see.' She pulls the card out of the front of my dress. 'Jesus. I bet he's got a whole load of these. Look – he's written them out beforehand. So he can pass them out to girls he gets off with. What an arse.'

'Give it back,' I say, and I grab it and tuck it in my bag.

Liz stops dead and glowers at me. 'Fliss, you did want to be rescued didn't you?'

'Yeah,' I slur. 'Yeah . . . thanks.'

'Only we ought to go. It's late, and there's been a fight outside –'.

'A fight?'

'Load of lads. Someone got bottled. The police've been.'

'Where's Meg?'

'She went outside to call a cab on her mobile. The reception in here is crap.'

We get outside into the cold night air, and see Meg, standing safely by a bouncer. She waves frantically. By her feet, there's a big streak of oily red blood. 'We've got to go round the corner,' Meg calls out, urgently. 'The cabbie says he won't stop outside the club, says he doesn't want to land in the middle of any trouble.'

'There won't be any more trouble tonight, ladies,' says the huge bouncer, with relish. 'We got it sorted.'

'Yeah, but – the cabbie's bothered about the police. He said to wait round there.'

'OK, ladies, but you take care, won't you. Make sure it's the cab you ordered before you hop inside it, right?'

'God,' mutters Liz, as we totter round the corner, 'all we wanted was a good night out . . .'

We get round the corner and stop dead. There's a group of girls there, six or seven of them, tough, mean-looking girls, some of them hefty, some of them spike-thin, all with their hair pulled tight back and these baggy clothes on.

'Blimey,' breathes Meg, 'I'm not waiting anywhere near *them*.'

There's something going on. The gang of girls are standing in a circle, jostling and pushing each other. As I stare I realise it's not each other they're pushing about, it's another girl, standing rigid in the middle of them. She's got long loose hair and she's dressed very differently from them, and they're all focused on her, and she looks absolutely faint with fear.

'Look,' the biggest girl is snarling, 'I ain't interested in what you need it for. We need it.'

'Yeah, look at you, you stuck-up bitch. With your mobile phone.'

'Get that off 'er an' all, Tonya.'

'Yeah. Basically, you're goin' to hand your money over – or you're goin' to get done. Your decision.'

'Need a bit of time to make your mind up, do ya?' sneers the biggest girl. 'OK. Ten . . . nine . . . eight . . .'

And all the other girls join in the slow countdown, jeering and menacing. It's something they must do, something they're used to doing. For a second I think, insanely, of me, Meg and Liz counting down before we drink our tequila. Counting down to add to the excitement, to the sense of occasion.

Counting down to make sure we all act at the same time.

'Five ... four ...'

'Jesus,' says Meg. 'We'd better get the bouncer!' And she sprints off round the building but Liz and I don't move, we can't, we're frozen, transfixed.

'Two ... ONE!' they chant. And then there's just the briefest of sick pauses – and then they pitch in. One of them shoves the long-haired girl hard, so she staggers back against another girl, who grabs her hair and yanks it. A third lifts her boot and kicks out, hard, a fourth swings her fist, and the long-haired girl crumples, buckles like a broken doll, and falls to the ground. Then they're on her like dogs, like jackals.

And, watching, I start to shake, really shake, from my guts outwards, right to my hands, right to my feet. I'm shaking with pure rage. And then, somehow, I'm moving. Moving forward, racing forward, screaming, 'She's on her own! You FUCKING BASTARDS! She's ON HER OWN!' I crash land into the nearest girl, fists flying. My fists make contact with a face, the side of a head ...

'Jesus, who's this fucking *nutter*?' Someone rams me, but I don't go over, I'm laying out all about me still, flailing like mad, like I'm so full of rage nothing and no one can stop me. I get kicked on the leg, I get punched on the back of the head, I can hear Liz screaming my name, I see her racing towards me, then someone slams me in the stomach and I go down, down on all fours, and then I lose it, everything goes black.

Twenty

I come to, lights like a motorway pile-up flashing through my half-closed eyes. 'She was,' I hear Liz saying tearfully, 'she was just trying to help!'

'Look Miss – they've all been fighting – I can't decide who to take in and who to leave here just on your say so –'

'But you've only got to look at her! That lot – they're a gang – they were beating up that girl – and Fliss pitched in –'

'I know this lot,' says a deep voice which I think belongs to the bouncer. 'Trouble. Nothing but trouble. Wouldn't let 'em in the club.'

'Pity you don't keep an eye on what goes on round the corner though, isn't it, sir?'

'I came!' the bouncer bellows. 'Soon as her friend yelled for me, I came and broke it up! Bloody girls,' he adds bitterly. 'More vicious than the lads nowadays.'

I hear the crackling of a police radio, robotic words coming out. 'She needs to be seen by a doctor,' someone's saying, all firm. 'We're taking the other one in to be seen.'

'She's OK,' says Meg, desperately. 'Fliss. *Fliss!* Say you're OK!'

I snap open my eyes. 'I'm OK,' I gasp. I stand up, flash them a bright smile. There's no way I'm going to get taken down to the police station, no way. 'I'm really OK. I just – there were about eight of them, it was a massacre, it was horrible...'

'You were very brave to pitch in,' says the policeman, doubtfully. 'I mean – daft, too, but then once you'd seen that poor girl in there on her own...'

'Is she going to be all right?'

'Yes. Nasty cut to the face needs stitching. But you passed out, then, miss. You should be checked for concussion.'

'I was winded, that's all.'

'She was only out for a second or so,' pleads Megan. 'You turned up just as she went down...'

The policeman puts his hand on my shoulder: tells me to keep both eyes on his index finger which he brings in towards my face, then away again. 'All right,' he says, finally. 'You three get off. That your cab, is it? You see her right to her front door, you two, won't you? And if you feel at all iffy, miss – call your doctor or the hospital. OK?'

The three of us hurry over to the cab and clamber gratefully inside, squashing ourselves side by side on the back seat. Then we shut the door and we're safe in the stale damp darkness.

'God, the pigs are everywhere on a Saturday night,'

grumbles the cabbie. 'And they all think they're in some bloody high-speed action film. Can't go up the road without some copper squealing past you with 'is lights flashing and 'is siren on. You all right back there? Doesn't one of you want to sit up front with me? No? OK – where we goin' then?' Meg cranks out my address, and the cabbie continues: 'You're lucky you've still got me, to be honest, ladies. I was goin' to move off once they roared up, but one of 'em told me to stay put, and in my business, if a copper tells you to stay put, you *stay* put...'

He rabbits on and on as we speed along the road, swerving to avoid the odd group of late-night drunks. 'I gave the police our names and addresses,' mutters Meg. 'But they said they doubted that girl would press charges...'

'Too scared,' says Liz, bitterly. There's a silence. We're all kind of shocked and sickened, numb with it. Then Liz whispers, 'You sure you're all right, Fliss?'

'Yeah. Fine. In fact I feel stone-cold sober now.'

'Maybe you should've got yourself checked out...it's just...if you got taken to the police station...'

'...it would put the fear of God into your folks and mine and we'd never be allowed out again. I'm fine, honestly. Just a bit bruised. In fact – it's my knuckles that hurt most.'

'Well, you really laid into them, didn't you?' She picks up my right hand and solemnly examines it in the uncertain light from the street lamps and passing cars. I look at it, too; it's puffy and red-looking and it's really starting to hurt. 'Blimey, Fliss,' she murmurs. 'That's bad. Move all your fingers?'

I waggle them, wincing.

'Not broken. God, though. You hooligan!' There's a tiny pause, then she says, 'I was coming to help, you know. Just as you went down. But then that bouncer pitched in, thank God, and the police arrived just about the same time ... they did this amazing U-turn, right in the middle of the road. I thought they were going to run down the whole lot of us.'

'Well I reckon that gang could've taken the bouncer, so it's a good job the feds were so close.'

'Yeah,' she laughs, all rueful. 'One advantage of clubbing in a dodgy district. Look, I ... I should've pitched in sooner. It's just – I couldn't move. I couldn't believe what I was seeing – I couldn't believe what you were doing.'

I laugh, take my hand back. 'Neither could I,' I say.

There's no noise in the house when I let myself in. Mum usually waits up for me, or she wakes when she hears my key in the door and calls out muggily 'You all right, Fliss?' But this time there's no sound. I go quietly up the stairs and up to her bedroom door, then I push it open and peer round. The room's pitch black because the street light outside the house has switched off. I can just make out her shape underneath the duvet. A hunched shape, a lonely shape. She's breathing very, very slowly, deeply asleep. I get this lump in my throat – I want to wake her up, climb into bed beside her like I used to when I was tiny, tell her about the fight, tell her about Simon, tell her about everything.

'Mum,' I whisper. 'Mum?'

She doesn't move. There's an empty wine glass beside the bed, and I can smell a sharp, sour, winey smell in the room. She's been drinking more over the last weeks, I know that, and I can't blame her.

I just wish she'd wake up for me.

I walk out, go into my bedroom, shut the door. I feel hyper, like my head's got a whole swarm of killer bees buzzing around inside it. It must be the adrenalin or something, because of the fight. All the alcohol I've drunk has spun off to the outer edges of my brain and in the centre of it my mind is very clear. I don't feel the least bit like sleeping.

I go over to the full–length mirror screwed to the wall next to my bed, and examine my face in it. The damage isn't too bad. My top lip's slightly swollen, that's all, and there's a graze on my forehead but it's hidden by my hair. Carefully, I feel the back of my head, sketching my fingers over the big lump that's starting to form. That's my worse injury, I reckon. That, and what I've done to my hands. I look down at them, and I remember the way I smashed my fist into the side of that big girl's stupid face. I can't help it, I start to smile. I felt so good when I was doing that. Like I didn't have to think any more, just act. Like all the angst inside me had found an escape, it was shooting out, like a boil bursting, leaving me clean and mended.

O Jesus, what does that mean? Am I becoming like them, those gang girls? Some kind of psychopath who finds peace through beating the crap out of someone? Maybe that's all those girls were after – a bit of relief from what was going on inside them. Maybe they need to do what they do, to stop them going mad.

I draw closer to the mirror, examine my swelling mouth, and I find myself thinking about Clary Andover.

She was in the year below us at school – she left last term. There was a big scandal surrounding her, because she kept turning up with these cuts on her arms. She told a few of her friends that her big brother was doing it with a knife, to force her to hand over money, and just because he enjoyed it, because he was a sadist. Her form teacher got involved, he wanted to call the police, he wanted to get the brother arrested and stuff. It was only right at the last moment that Clary broke down and admitted that she was the one who'd been doing it all along, not her brother – she'd been slicing into her own arms. And I remember that at the time there was this sense, almost, of anti-climax and relief, like it was OK if it was her doing it, as if it wasn't nearly so bad. She had to leave the school, and get proper treatment. People talked a bit about why she felt she had to hurt herself, how it didn't make any sense, but then they forgot about her.

I hold up my hands to the mirror, examine them in the reflection. They don't look like my hands – they're more swollen now, the knuckles grazed and bloody. What was good when I was hitting out? Hurting that girl or just hurting me? I could've been hitting anything. I could've been hitting a brick wall.

I think about Clary Andover and I suddenly know that it was far, far scarier that it was her, and not her brother, who was cutting her arms.

Twenty-one

Sunday, getting on for midday, and I've only just made it out of the bathroom, wet from my shower, and Mum still isn't up. She calls out to me from her room in this sickly, quavery voice.

'Yeah?' I ask, and peer into her room. 'You want a cuppa tea?'

'Oh, yes. Yes please.'

'What's the matter? Did you go on a blinder or something?'

Mum looks up at me from her bed, all pleading. She's got great rings of mascara round her eyes where she didn't clean it off the night before; it makes her look really haggard. 'I lost it,' she wheezes. 'I got the girls to bed and I opened a bottle of wine and sunk it. Then I opened another. Then – oh, *God* – I opened another. I forgot to eat. I feel dreadful.'

I don't answer. I suppose I feel pretty hungover too but it's OK, it's manageable, it's just part of the whole way I'm feeling.

'Are the girls up?' Mum asks.

'Yeah. Telly's on.'

'Oh, God – I hate them watching telly all morning –'

'Mum, I hardly think that's a major concern, do you? Not with –' I trail off and wave my hand at her, at the bed.

'No, OK. Oh, God, Fliss, I'm sorry but I can't move. I feel dreadful. I tried to make myself sick last night, but I couldn't, I've never been able to...'

I close my eyes. I don't want to hear.

'Could you hold the fort for me, darling? If I get a couple more hours' sleep I'm sure I'll be fine. I'll be... uuurgh, oh God, I feel like I've got alcohol poisoning or something...'

'Go back to sleep,' I mumble. 'I'll bring some tea up later.'

'They'll've got themselves some cereal,' she says. 'If you could just make them sandwiches or something for lunch ...and maybe go with them to the park or something...just a bit of fresh air...'

'OK,' I mutter.

'It was seeing him,' she suddenly spits out. 'Having to face *him*, all pleased with himself getting back from Bales Farm, the ideal dad, with his daughters all smeary with jam from their cream tea, all tired and happy, clutching those little bags from the souvenir shop with their pencils with a sheep on top...Phoebe's was a sheep, Alexa's was a bull...they were so happy, he'd made them happy, and all it took was a couple of fucking pencils...' Tears are rolling down her face, mixing with the mascara streaks. I stare at her, horrified. I think – this isn't her, it isn't. Maybe she has got alcohol poisoning.

'I wanted to kill him,' she raves on. 'All smug and bonded with his little girls, and then getting in his car, *our* car, our main car, going back to his *mistress* –'

I can't bear any more. 'Mum, get some sleep,' I whisper. I start to walk out of the room. 'Get some sleep, Mum.'

For the next few hours, I go through the motions with Phoebe and Alexa. I tell them Mum's got a tummy upset, and they have to turn the telly off now and we'll go to the park and work up an appetite for lunch. Phoebe's quite happy, pleased I'm being nice to them for once, probably. Alexa isn't fooled though. Her eyes have got that hunted, haunted look permanently now. Like she wants to know but daren't ask. And her fingernails are bitten down so far the quicks are sore and bleeding.

They haven't said anything about my mouth looking puffy and bruised. It fits in with the way we're all looking, I suppose. Swollen eyed, puffy and bruised.

I don't think about the fight, not any more. It's like I've just moved on from it. All the time I'm watching the girls on the swings, though, I'm thinking of that word Mum used. Mistress. It's crazy. Someone as starched up and chalky-skinned and ramrod straight as my dad can't have a *mistress*. Mistresses wear silk and seductive perfume and they don't have to work their arses off and they put love first . . . that sort of woman wouldn't be with Dad. She wouldn't.

When I think about her, this mistress, all the tightness comes back inside me, all the pressure, gagging up into my throat. It's unbearable. I'm trying to be normal, trying to interact with the girls, but I feel disconnected, like we're all in a film, and I'm acting badly, I'm totally fake.

Mum still isn't up when I get home. I make a big fuss about getting bread out of the bin and asking the girls whether they want cheese or tuna in their sandwiches. Alexa wants to go up and see Mum but I say – 'Let me take her some tea up, make sure she's awake.' I'm not sure Mum can cope with putting on a front for Alexa just yet.

When I trudge up with the tea she is awake, propped up on one elbow. She looks a bit better; she's drawn the curtains half back. 'Thanks, darling,' she mutters, taking the tea from me with a shaky hand. 'God, Fliss, I'm so sorry. I feel so ashamed of myself.'

'Why should you be? It's *him* who ought to be ashamed.'

'Maybe. But I've got to cope. I've got to look after things here.'

'You will,' I say.

'I do feel better. I'll get up in a minute – Alexa needs help with that history project –'

'Yeah. Mum?'

'Yes love?'

'I'm going out tonight.'

'On a Sunday?'

'Yes. I've . . . I've got to. Just for a couple of hours.'

Mum heaves a sigh, and puts her mug of tea down on the bedside table. 'OK,' she murmurs.

As soon as I get downstairs I grab my bag and go into the front room, where I can phone in private. I find the card that sleazy guy gave me last night at the club. Dale it says – his name's Dale. That figures. Before I can stop and think I've punched out his number.

Four rings, and then a woman answers. I put on this slangy, hard voice and ask to speak to Dale. She shouts for him, and soon he's breathing into the receiver. 'Yeah?'.

'Hi. It's me, from last night. The girl in the blue top you bought a tequila sunrise for.'

There's a pause, but before it gets long enough to be really insulting he says, 'Oh – yeah! I remember. I gave you my number, didn't I?'

Obviously, I think, while I say: 'Yeah. Did you mean it?'

'Mean what?'

'About phoning you up if I fancied going out for a drink?'

'Sure. That'd be great. Hey – I remember you. The one with the aggressive friend who dragged you off home.'

'Yeah. I was really pissed off with her.'

'Yeah? Wanted to stay did you?'

'I was enjoying myself,' I say, in this sultry voice that nearly makes me throw up when I hear it leave my mouth. But it has the right effect.

'Me, too, sweetheart. Well – when you wanna meet up then?'

I take in a deep breath and say, 'Tonight.'

'Tonight? It's Sunday!'

'I know. What's the matter – you deeply religious or something?'

He laughs. 'No. Just I have work the next day.'

'Well I've got . . . college.' No point in saying 'school'. No point telling him how young I am.

'Yeah, but . . .' He's hesitating, wondering if he wants to bother. I can hear it. 'I bet you haven't got to get up at six-thirty, like I have.'

'Oh, OK. Forget it. It's just – oh, God. I need to get out, see someone different, you know? It's all got so weird – I got in a fight last night and –'

'A *fight*? Who with?'

'These horrible girls. A gang of them.'

'Blimey. You all right?'

'Yeah, I'm OK. It's just it's – I wanna get out tonight, that's all.'

I haven't said much, but it's enough. Because what I've really said is I'm desperate, on the edge, and that's enough for him. He's caught the bait.

'Oh, OK, why not?' he says. 'It'd be great to meet up. No reason we can't meet early, is there? Have a drink, have a nice chat. Shall I pick you up? I got a bike.'

'A motorbike?'

'Yeah. I wasn't offering to stick you on my handlebars, darlin'!'

I force out a giggle, and say, 'My mum'd have a fit if a bike rolled up. Look – what about The Cat and Fiddle? Over by The Ridgeway – you know, that big new estate? That's near me. Meet you in there?'

'Sure. I know it. Eight o'clock OK?'

'I'll be there,' I say, and I put the phone down.

And then I wait, but all the time there's this fear and excitement because of meeting Dale, this stranger, in six, then four, then two hours' time . . . I don't worry about it, about the risks I'm taking. I don't think he's older, bigger, stronger and I don't know him at all and he groped me pretty badly at the club. Well, I do – but I don't care. As I'm getting ready to go out I think about Clary Andover again. This date, I think – it's my version of cutting into my arm. This anxiety, this fear I'm feeling right now – it's taking the misery away. And he's going to be like the knife slicing into me, stopping me feeling what I'm feeling.

Twenty-two

I leave the house about half past seven, because it's a fair walk to the pub. I've made sure I've put loads of club-type make-up on, so Dale will recognise me from last night. He needs to, because I'm not at all sure I'm going to recognise him. I keep trying to pull a picture of him into my mind, but I can't.

I slink into the pub car park at five past eight. Two motorbikes are standing there, near to each other but not together. One of them's got to be his.

I hate going into pubs on my own, but I do it. The way my heart pounds is OK, it's a better way to be than normal. I walk slowly over to the bar, and I'm scanning everyone, looking for guys on their own. Not that brown-haired one over there, in the cream-coloured jacket. No, Dale was taller, a bit tough-looking. Like that one there – but he's with his mates.

I've reached the bar. What the hell am I going to do now? I can't order a drink, I look too young. I walk on over to the other side of the pub. My legs are all stiff with embarrassment, I'm moving like a robot. I've gone as far as I can go, right up to the toilets on the far side. And then the door to the Gents swings open, and this hard-looking bloke walks out and stops dead. He puts his head on one side, frowns and smiles at me at the same time, raises his hand and points. 'Are you –?'

'Dale?' I squeak.

'Yeah. Yeah, *hi*.' And he's by my side, one arm round me already, squeezing me, all god-isn't-this-good. 'You won't believe this, but I forgot your name. I feel like a real twat.'

We never got as far as swapping names, I think. 'Fliss,' I say.

'Fliss. That's cute. That short for –?'

'Felicity.'

'Blimey. Posh, ay?'

'Not really.'

'You want a drink? Tequila, wasn't it?' He smirks at me, as if remembering what I drank gives him extra merit points or something.

'Just a lager, please.'

And he's swaggering over to the bar, still with his arm round me, calling to the barman, all confident and pulling a roll of notes out of the back pocket of his jeans. It must be weird, being that confident, knowing the barman's more intimidated by you than you are by him. He gets me one of those trendy lagers in a bottle, and no glass, and a pint of beer for himself, then he steers me over to a little table in the corner, and soon we're sitting side by side, and he hasn't taken his arm from round my shoulders the whole time.

'Well, I'm glad you phoned me, Felicity,' he says. 'Cheers.' He clinks his glass against my bottle spilling beer on my hand, but he doesn't notice. 'Not too keen on this pub, as it happens,' he goes on. 'Full of wankers.' He takes a long pull at his beer.

My heart's still thudding. He slams down his glass and I look at his mouth sideways, and remember the way it ground into mine last night, and I can't decide if I feel turned on by the thought or if I hate it, and then I decide it doesn't really matter which.

I can't just sit there like an idiot, though, can I. I've got to talk to him. 'What do you do?' I ask weakly.

'What do I do? You mean like my job?'

'Yeah.'

'Oh, Christ, let's not talk about that.' He pulls me up against him. 'It's still the weekend, right?'

'Right.'

'And we deserve a bit of fun before the grind sets in again, yeah?'

I laugh uneasily. I can't keep my eyes off his mouth. He hasn't shaved round it properly, and there's all this black stubble under his bottom lip. I pick up my bottle of lager, lift it to take a drink, and as I do he catches sight of my hand. 'Christ, you *did* get in a fight, didn't you?' He sounds half disgusted, half turned on. 'Bit of a wildcat are you?'

I shrug. 'I don't make a habit of it.'

'Glad to hear it, Felicity.'

'It's just – you know. Things've been weird.'

'What things?'

'Oh, I dunno. My mum and dad – they're getting a divorce, and –'

'Oh, *that*. Bummer. Yeah – my old man walked out. Six – seven years ago.'

'Did you . . . were you really upset?'

'Nah. Glad to see the back of him.'

There's a silence, and Dale takes another swig of his beer. That conversation seems to be over, and I can't think of any way of starting up another one. 'So – what you want to do?' he demands. 'Go to a club?'

I have this sudden awful picture of him backing me into a wall in a dark corner of the club, and anyway, I've thought this one out already. I know where I'm going to ask him to take me.

'Well – I sort of said I'd drop in on this friend,' I mutter.

'Yeah?' he says, unenthusiastically.

'Yeah. She's got a free house. She's sort of having a party – just a small one –'

'Sounds OK. Where is it?'

Then I take a deep breath and say, 'Magpie Place. You know – those new flats? Bridge Street.'

'I know 'em,' he says, and he downs the last of his beer and stands up.

Twenty-three

Soon we're out in the pub car park and heading for the shiniest of the two bikes. He's got a spare helmet, and as he straps it under my chin he ducks his head right down close to mine and breathes beer smell straight into my face. He's looking at me, all summing-me-up, all deliberate and corny and sexy, and I think for a minute he's going to fix his mouth onto mine, but he doesn't.

'All right, Felicity,' he says. 'Let's go.' He swings his leg over the bike and straddles it, macho-style, posing like that old *Easy Rider* poster. 'On you get.'

Everything he says is in this teasing, challenging, I-know-you voice. It's like he's playing with me, like a cat with a mouse, and it's half sexy and half sick-making. 'Come on, Felicity,' he repeats. I put my hands on his shoulders, and swing up behind him. I've only ever been on a bike once before, and that was all safe, driven by a friend of my uncle's. But I know what to do.

He kicks the engine into action. 'Magpie Place, Bridge Street, yeah?' he shouts, over his shoulder.

'That's right,' I say. That's right – Dad's new home. I remembered it because when I read it on that scrap of paper Mum chucked down, I had a really vivid picture of an evil-looking magpie, clucking and cackling on an old, broken-down bridge.

Dale kicks the bike into life, and we roar off along the road. The bike judders and jerks underneath me. Air rushes past, black and frosty on my face. I'm behaving like a lunatic, I know it. Trusting my life to someone I only met last night. We could crash and die. Or he could take me off anywhere, tie me up and rape me and murder me. I don't care though. The speed and the wind ripping past are all I feel. That and the fear. I'm drowning in it. It doesn't matter where he takes me – Bridge Street or the back of a truck or a wood somewhere – it's all a disaster, it's all the knife cutting out the misery.

We're on a deserted road now, skeleton trees breaking up the light from the street lamps. Dale slows the bike, curses, does a sudden U-turn, then slows again and stops. 'That must be it,' he shouts, pointing to some big open gates. 'Can hardly see the sign in this light.'

He legs the bike over to the gates, stops to the side of them, and turns the engine off. Then he pulls his helmet off and turns to me. 'So,' he demands. 'What flat is it then?'

Stick shadows from the trees waving in front of the street light fall over his face, making him look ugly, scarred. He's frowning – his good mood's gone. Maybe he was having second thoughts on the way over. Maybe he's thinking I'm not really worth it, I'm not worth the effort.

'I'm not sure,' I say. 'My friend said we'd find it by the noise.'

'Well I can't hear any music,' he says impatiently. 'Not exactly rocking, is it?'

'It was only going to be a small party.'

'Shouldn't we've got some drink or something?'

'It'll be OK,' I say, and I pull off my helmet and hand it to him, then I start walking towards the lit-up entrance hall of the flats because I don't know what else to do.

I peer through the big glass doors. Inside there's a fake-looking tree in a blue tub, and lift doors to the left. Dale comes up behind me, too close. 'Are those doors open?' he barks.

I pull on the doors, knowing they'll be locked, and they are. There's a line of lit-up buzzers on the wall beside me, all with names by them. 'Can't you find her name?' he moans.

I read the names, one by one. One of them will be hers. One of them will be Dad's mistress. My eyes dig into them, trying to find her.

'Come on, which is it?' snaps Dale impatiently.

I turn to him, grip my lower lip in my teeth in this 'whoops-silly-me' way that I hope to God he finds endearing. 'I can't remember,' I bleat. 'I can't remember her surname. Thing is – she's really only a friend of a friend. Liz said she'd be here about ten. What time is it?'

He looks at his watch. 'Nine-fifteen,' he says, sourly.

'Maybe she'll be along a bit early. Or someone else will – someone going to the party.'

'Why don't you just start at the top, ring each buzzer?'

'What – and say is there a party in your flat?'

'Yeah, why not?'

'Oh, I can't,' I squeak. 'Really, I can't. Anyway, she's . . . she's not supposed to be having a party. And if I buzz everyone – the neighbours'll find out, won't they. Find out and tell her parents.'

Dale looks at me all hostile and huffs out a sigh. 'Look, Felicity. This is not exactly all happening, is it? What're we supposed to do till one of your friends who actually *knows* this bird turns up?'

He's going to say – let's go. He's going to suggest a pub, or a club. But I have to stay here, near Dad's new home. I have to.

I move up close to him, slip my hands inside the thick black leather of his jacket, slide them right round his waist. My face is so close to his now we're breathing in each other's air. It feels sick, it feels wrong, but I do it. 'Oh, come on, Dale,' I murmur. 'Let's wait. It's not so cold here, in this porch thing. Is it?'

I'm craning my head up towards him – my mouth's about ten centimetres away from his. He laughs, sneering, then he brings his face down to mine and I know I've got him.

I really turn it on. I mash my mouth against his, thrash my tongue around like a worm on a hook. He slides both his hands right down my back, pushes them up under my jacket and gets hold of my backside. I squirm with hating it, with the effort of making myself not push him away.

'Hey – calm down,' he murmurs. 'What you so frantic about?'

This is what made Dad leave. Sex. This is all it took. I hook my arm round Dale's neck, pull him down to me, start nibbling at his ear, and I'm so repulsed I make myself go further, I make myself stick my tongue right inside his ear, and I nearly gag with it, with the sharp, burning, alien taste.

Then I move down on to his neck.

'You are a little raver, aren't you?' he says, pushing me back. 'Leave off, I don't wanna lovebite.' He brings his hands round and casually undoes the three big buttons on my jacket. 'I'd never hear the end of it from my mates at work.'

He pushes up my jumper, squeezes me through my bra. My breathing's so fast now I think I'm going to choke any minute, and all I want is to push him off me, shove him off and run. But I don't. I get this sudden stab of memory, of Simon. How careful he was, how he'd never do anything unless he was sure I wanted it too, so much so I'd want to scream sometimes, I'd want us just to go for it, get carried away. Whatever we were doing, Simon and I never stopped being who we were, the people we were.

I don't feel like a person now. Dale's bringing his face down onto mine again, gnawing at me, and all the time his hands are moving, mauling.

So this is it, is it? This is what made Dad leave.

Suddenly a car drives in through the big open gates, headlights swinging over us, spot-lighting us. 'Shit,' snarls Dale. He lets my jumper slide back down. 'Maybe this is your mate.'

Two old people are crunching up the drive towards us, dumpy and solid in their winter coats. I press my face against Dale's leather jacket, blocking them out. They don't say anything, just unlock the glass doors with a clunking, whirring sound, but I can feel their disapproval, and I can feel Dale staring them out aggressively over the top of my head. Then the door shuts heavily behind them.

'I wish your mate'd hurry up,' Dale mutters. 'I'm getting fucking cold.' He shoves one hand up the back of my jumper and efficiently unhooks my bra. 'You're all right you are,' he murmurs into the top of my head. 'There gonna be a spare room at this party, ay?'

I feel like my flesh is crawling under his hands. In my head I see myself kneeing him, slamming him back against the wall, kicking his head apart as he slides to the ground. His hands have moved down now, down to the fastening on my jeans, like no part of me is good enough to keep his attention for more than a minute. 'Hey,' I gurgle, trying to sound soft, teasing, as I grab hold of his hand with all the strength I can muster, 'what you trying to do – totally undress me?'

'Oh, *come* on, Felicity.'

'No–oo! Not out here!'

He shakes my hand away, and I add, desperately, 'There'll be a room inside. I know there will.'

'Yeah, well, I'm not convinced about that. I'm not convinced we're ever gonna get into this party. *If* it's going on.'

And he starts in on me again. It's like torture. I'm writhing about with repulsion and he thinks it's because I'm turned on, because somehow I'm managing to act like I'm turned on, I'm even, somewhere inside me, trying to get turned on. I don't know what's going on. I just know I've got to keep him here. Just a bit longer.

He's going for my jeans fastening again and this time he makes it. I grab his hand with both of mine, and then, breaking through, I hear the voice I've been waiting for.

That I'm here for.

'Felicity? Felicity – what the hell are you *doing*?'

Twenty-four

Dale's hands drop away from me as though I'm suddenly electrified. I turn round and face Dad with all my clothes gaping.

'How did you know I was out here?' I demand.

'How did I –? What the hell does that matter? What on earth are you doing here?'

'I just wanted to see your new home, *Dad*.'

'But how did you – what –'

'Dad?' mutters Dale, disgustedly. 'What the fuck is going on here?'

Dad rounds on him. 'Who the hell are you?'

'This is Dale,' I spit. 'I met him last night.'

Dad takes in a deep breath. He looks battered, he looks like I've just smashed him round the face, and I'm glad.

'How did you know I was here?' I ask again.

'I was putting some rubbish down the chute,' he says

bitterly. 'I heard the people from the flat below grumbling to each other about this couple they'd just seen outside. They were going on about how young the girl was and how parents nowadays have no control.'

He lets out this angry, shaky sigh. Then he goes on, 'Anyway, call it a hunch – call it what you like – I came down to see.'

There's a pause. Then he says: 'For Christ's sake do your clothes up.'

At this, Dale finds his voice. 'I'm off,' he snarls. 'Nice game, Felicity. Enjoyed it. Next time you want to string someone along like that, don't call my number, OK?'

'Just clear off, will you?' says Dad.

'I'm going! Sweet daughter you got there, mate. That is one fucked up little psycho. Congratulations.' And he stamps off towards the gates and his motorbike, calling back over his shoulder, 'You want to sort your family out, mate, OK?'

Dad rounds on me. 'Look, Felicity. I don't know what you're playing at, bringing that *scum* here – how on earth did you know where I was anyway?'

'Why? Is it meant to be a secret?'

'No – it's just –'

'You don't want your family visiting you, that's it, isn't it?'

'Look – let me take you home. My car's over there, I'll –'

'No! I want to go inside! I want to see where you're living now! What's the matter, Dad – don't you want your own daughter to come to your new home?'

Dad glares at me, his mouth working silently. I glare back, fists clenched, heart pounding. Then there's the sound of Dale's bike roaring off into the night. And then, at Dad's shoulder, someone new appears.

She's nothing special – brown hair in a bob, quite tall. Younger than him. Of *course*. Just like Mum described.

'Martin?' she says. She's got this silly, soft, girly little voice. 'Is everything OK? Only I heard shouting and –'

'It's fine,' Dad barks. 'Look – you go in, love. I won't be long.'

When I hear him call her that, call her 'love', I think I'm going to start screaming.

She's looking at me. 'Oh, God, Martin. Is this –'

'Anita, please go in, will you?'

At the sound of her name, something inside me explodes, all bright and vivid, like a firework. I open my mouth wide to laugh. 'An – neet – ta!' I crow. 'Wow, is that your name? That's amazing – bit like Alexa, isn't it, Dad, like your *daughter*. Except it's got neat in it, and she looks neat, doesn't she, and I bet the flat's all neat, not like our messy old home that you couldn't stand –'

'Felicity, stop this,' groans Dad.

'Stop what? Aren't you going to introduce me properly, Dad? To your *mistress*?'

Anita's looking at me, and looking like she might faint at any minute. She opens her mouth, and nothing comes out. Then she squeaks, 'But how did she . . . how did she . . .'

'Find out? Find out where my dad had done a runner to? Meant to be a big secret, wasn't it, Dad? Well, someone told Mum. Someone at your office who thinks you're an absolute *bastard* told Mum. And she followed you here, and saw you. She told me all about it, all about An – neet – ta. Only actually – she was a bit flattering,

159

what she said.' I round on her. 'Look at you,' I spit, and my voice is so choked up with hate and loathing I can barely get the words out. 'I don't know what he sees in you. You don't look like a mistress. You're too fucking *ugly* and *ordinary* to be a mistress.'

Dad steps forward then and grabs hold of my arm. 'That's *enough*, Felicity. Come on, I'm driving you home.'

'No! I want to see your little love nest! I want to fucking *smash it up*!'

'Look — will you keep your *voice* down and stop *swearing* —'

I tear my arm away. I've got this rage storming through me like a great river, like freedom. 'Stop swearing? You walk out on your whole family and you're bothered about swearing? That's rich, that is. *Fucking* rich. You can't tell me what to do any more. You've walked out on all that. I can do what the fuck I like now. If you hadn't come down just then, I'd've done it with that bloke right there, we practically did it anyway, we —'

Dad grabs my arm again, yanks it down so hard my head snaps back and my teeth jolt together. 'What's wrong?' I scream at him, right in his face. 'You think you're the only one who can go off and shag who you like?'

He's dragging me along now, manhandling me over to where all these cars are parked. I know he wants to hit me, really hit me. Anita's peeping and squeaking behind us and we're both ignoring her. I think about hacking Dad in the shins as he hauls me along but I don't because of the way we're both ignoring Anita.

Dad unlocks our big family car, bundles me into the passenger seat, slams the door on me. Then he gets in beside me, at the wheel. It's all different now we're inside the car. It's quiet, still. Everyone else is shut out, the night's shut out, the cold and the wind. Dad's hunched over the wheel like he's ill. And I feel tired, tired, drained of everything inside me. Almost peaceful.

When I started out this evening I wasn't clear what I wanted. Just to stop the horrible cramped-in, twisted-up way I was feeling, to stop the horrible pressure building up inside me. I was striking out, at everyone, and at myself most of all, like Clary Andover with her knife.

It worked, though, didn't it. It was like I was mad, driven. And now I feel almost peaceful.

'Shall I take you back home?' Dad croaks.

I don't answer. He pushes the key into the ignition but he doesn't start up the engine. 'There was no need for that, you know,' he mutters.

'For what?'

'For that scene. It wasn't like you, Fliss. I've never seen you like that before. I mean – I can understand that you're angry. Of course I can. But things'll be sorted out quicker if . . . if –'

'If I don't make a scene?' I say, dully.

'I'm sorry you had to find out that way,' Dad goes on. 'Really sorry. Although I don't know what your mum was thinking of, getting in her car and following me like some – anyway. I was going to tell you – all of you. About Anita, I mean. I was just – I was waiting for the right time.'

I don't answer that. I'm hunched forward now, too, like Dad. He's holding the wheel and I'm hugging my knees.

'It was difficult enough just to talk about leaving,' he says. 'Your mum and I – we've barely spoken a civil word to each other since Christmas. And it's been bad, really

161

bad, for God knows how long before that. I couldn't've told her about Anita, not when things were so difficult, not when . . .'

He trails off, starts fiddling with the key in the ignition. Then he says, 'Look, let me drive you home, Felicity. We're both tired.'

'No,' I say.

'Now look – we can't sit here all night, can we?'

'I want to come up to your flat. I want to see where you're living now.'

'Look – I –'

'If you start the car up, I swear I'm going to open this door and jump out.'

He lets out a long, shuddering sigh, half despair and half anger. Then he says, 'Look, Felicity. I understand how upset you are, I really do. But I can't just take you up to the flat, not after you've . . . not after you've blown your top over Anita –'

'So you care more about how she's feeling than me, do you?'

Dad doesn't know how to take this. It's too raw, too ugly for him. I've never made demands like this of him before, never.

'I just think now is not the time,' he mutters.

'It is,' I snap. 'It *is*. I've come all this way, Dad. Look – I'm not going to "blow my top" again. I just want to see.'

There's a thick pause. Then he says, 'All right then. If you insist. But it's not my flat, it's –'

'I know, I know, it's hers.' I open the door, swing my legs out into the cold. 'Don't worry – I won't break anything.' I start walking towards the big glass doors, leaving Dad to follow me.

Twenty-five

And soon we're standing side by side, going up in the narrow carpeted lift. Our faces are multiplied all the way round by the mirrors on the walls. I look at Dad's reflection, but it won't meet my eyes. The lift slumps to a stop. 'Come on then,' he mutters.

Outside the lift there's a phony Greek vase on a stand with two identical cream-coloured front doors on either side of it. Dad steps over to the door on the left, puts a key in the lock, and opens it. Then he stands in the doorway, blocking it, and I can hear him hissing, 'Anita! *Anita!*' and then there's more hissing and whispering and I'm left standing in the corridor in front of the horrible phony Greek vase.

Dad turns back towards me, says, 'All right, Felicity, come on. Come in,' and he walks in through the door and I follow him.

We go through a tiny hall straight into a large open room like an illustration in a catalogue for bland, beige furniture. There's no sign of Anita.

She's in the kitchen, that room over there with the door nearly shut, I know she is. She's in there listening.

'Sit down,' Dad says wearily, and I sit down on the beige sofa.

I think about demanding to be given a guided tour, but I don't, I can't. Inside me, I feel like the pressure's starting up again, like a fist tightening. And I don't want it to; I can't bear it.

'D'you want a cup of tea?' Dad asks.

I shrug. My eyes are scouring the room. There's one of those naff telly cabinets in the corner and, at the window, curtains with a pattern so pale and boring you can't describe it. Underneath the posh-looking desk sits Dad's briefcase, the briefcase I've seen night after night dumped down among the schoolbags and trainers in the hall of our house. It makes me feel really weird, seeing it there.

There's a rattle in the kitchen; Anita must be making tea.

I want to see the bedroom. I want to see it.

Dad gets to his feet, heads for the kitchen, waits by the nearly shut door for a bit, then manoeuvres a tray through it, barely opening it any further. It makes me want to laugh. 'I'm not going to attack her,' I say. 'She can come out.'

'I don't think now's the time,' says Dad, and he comes over and puts the tray on the neat little coffee table in front of the sofa. Anita's laid out the whole works: teapot, cups, saucers, milk jug, even a sugar bowl. Anyone else would've just made two mugs and called out, 'How many sugars?' I look at the neat tea tray and I want to tip it up,

I want to pick it up and tip it all over Dad. The pressure inside me is getting worse.

'Where's the bathroom?' I say.

'What?'

'I need the bathroom.'

He doesn't answer for a moment, then he nods towards the door next to the kitchen. I stand up, walk over, go inside, click the bolt to.

It's very luxurious. Far more luxurious than our bathroom at home. Shiny tiles, shiny bath, soft blue towels and a soap dish like a crystal shell. I pick up a flowery make-up bag peer inside, pull out a lipstick, open it. Nasty, bright-enough pink. I want to smash it against the tiles, scrape and smear it all over the tiles, but I don't. I feel helpless. All the bravery running through me earlier has trickled away. I don't know what to do.

I sit down on the edge of the bath for what seems like ages, then I stand up and open the little pine-edged cupboard that's hanging on the wall, and then I just stand and stare inside. I can see the high-tech vitamin pills Dad always gets and Mum always grumbles about the expense of. Used to grumble about the expense of. I can see a man's deodorant between a blue perfume bottle, all curved and expensive-looking, and a jar of jojoba body cream.

I can see a packet of contraceptive pills.

'Come on out, Felicity,' says Dad's voice from the other side of the door. 'What are you doing in there?'

'Nothing,' I call back. 'I'm coming.'

I flush the toilet, run the tap. Then I leave the bathroom and sit back down on the sofa. Dad's poured the tea out – he hands me a cup. It rattles in the saucer as I hold it but I can't stop it shaking.

'I'm sorry,' I say. 'I'm sorry I made a scene. I'll just drink this and ...'

'I'll drive you home,' says Dad, gratefully.

'Yeah.'

There's a long pause, while we both sip our tea. I know Anita's still in the kitchen, scared to come out, ear pressed to the door probably, but I don't care, not now. And then Dad suddenly says: 'You do know Anita isn't the reason I left, don't you?'

I gawp at him, not answering. Then I croak, 'What difference does that make?'

'It's just – I don't want you to blame her. For me going.'

I can feel my whole face jump, contort. The fist inside me, grips, tightens. 'What the hell does it matter whether I blame her or not?' I spit.

'Because ... I want things to work out with her. I want you to get on together.'

'You want me to get on with the woman you've walked out on us for?'

'Felicity, I just told you, it wasn't her –'

'Her! Her! What about *me*? Why don't you care about *me*?'

He sits there, glaring ahead of him, stunned. He can't think what to say. My own father can't think what to say when I ask him to care about me. He's shocked, more shocked than he was by me cursing and swearing at him half an hour ago.

'Look,' he says carefully, still staring straight ahead, 'you're tired. Overwrought. Why don't I drive you back home now and ...'

' ... and then you can forget about me again, can't you? Like you always do.'

He sighs. He sounds weary, fed up.

And with that sigh, suddenly I lose it. Suddenly, I'm on my feet and I'm shouting and screaming things I'd pushed right down inside me years ago.

I'm screaming things I never even knew I *thought*.

'You forgot about me as soon as Alexa came along didn't you? She was the baby – she was your main concern! I can remember you saying it! "Come on, Felicity, you've had me all to yourself for six years, you've got to learn to share now." And I did share – and I shared when Phoebe was born, I was the big sister always there to help take care of them, and I thought – I *thought* once they got older, and more independent, maybe you and I could have a relationship again, maybe you'd have a bit of time for me and we could talk together again, maybe you'd bother to find out what I was up to, what I was *doing* with my life –'

Dad's looking at me absolutely appalled. 'Flissy,' he groans, 'I've always cared about you ...'

'When do you show it? How do you show it? You think walking out on me shows it?'

'I haven't walked out on you ...'

'Yes you have!'

'It's Mum and I that've split up, not –'

'You don't *live* with us any more! That's the truth of it, whatever you say! When will I see you, now? You see the girls, you take them swimming and stuff but –'

'Felicity, you didn't want to come! And that time I took the girls out for a pizza – you didn't want to come!'

'I know I didn't! But what else is there? What is there for *me*?'

There's a pause. I can practically see his mind racing, making the vein on his forehead pulse like crazy. 'Look,' he murmurs, 'it's difficult. I mean you and I – for the last few years – we haven't been close, have we. Teenage daughter and stodgy old dad, there in the background. I didn't suggest anything just for you because – well, it feels a bit false to suddenly start spending lots of time together, just because your mum and I have split up . . .'

So that's how you feel, is it, Dad? That's how you feel. I feel absolutely cold. So cold it's like all the blood has drained from my face.

'But, well . . .' he mumbles on, 'there's nothing to stop us making a change, is there? You say you hope we can have a bit more of a relationship, well, that's . . . that's lovely. Maybe when things have settled down a bit, and we've got over this bad patch, we can . . .'

He trails off. And suddenly, I feel really sickened – at me, him, everything. If I have to ask for his love like this I don't want it, it's too shameful, it's humiliating. Anything he offers now is sad, false. I don't want it.

The fist inside me is so tight now I can't breathe. The horrible, coiled thing I've been fighting so hard to keep down, to keep controlled – it's coming out. I drop the teacup, drop it straight down onto the beige carpet and race for the door of the flat. I pull it open and keep running. And I start crying, blubbering crazily as I lurch along. I'm not crying for Dad, for what he said, or what he didn't say. I'm crying for this father I never had who'd *know* me, who'd know who I was and love me for it.

I reach the end of the corridor. There's a big swing door at the end with 'Fire Escape' on it. I wrench it

open and see the staircase and my mind swoops and
gives way and as I slip my legs give way too and I fold
in on myself, and my head seems to smash and that's it.

Twenty-six

After that, I disappear from school for a long time, too, just like Clary Andover, the girl who used to cut her arms to get relief.

I'm in hospital for nine days. Observation for the bad cut on my head that I sustained slipping on the stairs, and for my concussion. Observation for my mental state because of how weird I am when I come round from the concussion. 'Breakdown', that's what they're saying. Breaking up, breakdown, broken.

People visit me in hospital. Dad, of course, but I can't speak to him, I feel too ashamed. He keeps telling me how bad he feels, over and over again. 'When I found you,' he says, 'I thought you'd tried to throw yourself down those stairs.'

Throwing myself down had gone through my mind, just for a split second. And then something had stopped me right at the last, something closed me down.

Dad's still living at Magpie Place. Even if I had thrown myself down the stairs, I don't think it would have been enough to make Dad leave Anita.

Mum visits too, of course. For two hours each day, although I ask her not to. On her own, and with the girls. Crying over me, concerned. Not understanding, wanting to know why. I can't really talk to her; I don't know how to explain. Phoebe and Alexa bring me cards they've made and stare at me with huge, empty-looking eyes, the way they stared at Dad the day he left home. All the time I feel how much I've let them all down, how much I've failed them, but I can't say anything.

Liz comes twice, once with Megan and once on her own. They don't ask me any questions. They're bright and chatty and don't really know what to say to me. They tell me the gossip, talk about what we're all going to do together when I'm better. It feels fake; I'm sure it feels fake to them too.

I'm given quite a few pills the first few days in hospital, and because of them it's like I'm behind a glass wall, watching people talk at me. I know somewhere I'm glad they care, glad they've come, but I can't really feel it. Then the nurses ease the pills off, and things get a bit harder, a bit more painful, and then, a few days before I leave hospital, I have a new visitor.

Her name's Jill, and she's very quiet and easy and ordinary. Her job is to let me talk. I don't want to at first; I won't say much. But she keeps sitting there, and she turns up the next day. We start slowly, piecing it all together. Why other kids can cope with the breakdown of their family, but I couldn't. Why I felt like I had to be the strong one in the family, when what I'd done proved I was the weakest – although Jill said I mustn't think like that. How I feel about Dad finding someone new. How it's weird, because I always thought it would be Mum who found someone new.

I realise, as I stumble along trying to explain things to her, that we'd never really talked at home about what was happening, and I realise how bad that was.

It's when I talk to her about Simon that I have what she calls my first 'breakthrough'. It all falls into place so clearly, the way I used him, the way I tried to make him be what he couldn't be, give me everything I was missing at home, all the security and attention I needed but wasn't getting. I feel so bad, thinking about Simon, and everything I put him through. I start to write a letter to him, apologising for everything, but I tear it up.

Then the morning before I'm due to leave hospital Mum brings in a card from him. It's been sent to our house. It has flowers and 'Get Well Soon' on the outside, and inside, just 'Simon'.

I think of him in the shop, choosing the card. I know he'd've spent ages worrying over which one to buy, and afterwards, he'd've spent ages trying to think what to write before deciding just to write 'Simon'. I don't cry when I first read it, when Mum's there, but later, just as they're settling the ward down for the night, I pick it up and read it again, and cry buckets into my pillow. The nurse has to come and change it, it gets so wet.

When I leave hospital and get back home, everything's different. For a start, Alexa seems to have grown up by years. There's a strength about her, a calmness I don't remember. Not quite as if she's taken my place as Mum's support, but almost.

Another difference is, Mum doesn't seem to need the support she once did. She's dealt with a lot of things, too; sorted stuff out with Dad about money and everything. The catering company is going well, and Jan's round at our house a lot of the time. They talk everything through while they chop and mix stuff. Their friendship is immense. There's a different balance in the house, but after a week or so at home I begin to see it's a good balance. Sometimes I wander into the kitchen and sit down and Jan asks me all upfront about how I'm feeling and I tell her. Mum listens, and encourages me to talk. It's easier, somehow, talking about it that way, with both of them there. It's good.

No one talks about me going back to school, though. I have all of February off, then we get into March. I don't want to talk about school, or GCSEs. I feel exhausted just by the thought. I see Jill twice a week and she tells me: we'll cross that bridge when you're ready for it.

Jill's office is on the other side of town. Mum drives me there, leaves me, and picks me up an hour later. On my second session there, I get really angry. 'We're just going round in circles!' I explode. 'All these questions – what good are they doing? I need help, don't I?'

'Do you?' she says.

'Yes!'

'What for?'

'Oh – God! It's obvious isn't it? To make sure I act like a normal person, get a hold of myself, get some kind of control over my life...'

'Well – OK, Fliss. But I'm not too hot on helping people act. Or control things.'

'Oh for Christ's sake – you're just – you're nit-picking over the words I used! You know what I mean.'

She leaves a long pause then and I get so irritated I get to my feet and spit out, 'I don't know what I'm doing here! You haven't got any answers!'

And what she says is: 'No, I haven't.'

I'm so surprised I sit down again. And then she goes on, with huge kindness, 'Fliss, I haven't got the answers, *you* have. What I'm going to do – if you want me to – is give you a bit of help digging around inside yourself and finding them.'

Pretty soon after that the hour's up, and the next day I find myself looking forward to the next session.

Twenty-seven

On my fifth visit to Jill's office, she says she wants to take things on to the next stage. She wants me to talk about everything that happened the night I went round to Dad's new home.

I baulk at first, because in my head that night's a black space, a no-go area. But she gets me to talk about how I phoned Dale, how I met him at the pub. Once I start I'm surprised by how easy it is; it seems like so long ago now, like it happened to someone else. We even end up laughing about how gross and pushy he was. Then I tell her all about what happened when Dad came out of the flats, and Anita followed him. That's harder to tell, but I manage it.

'It felt so good,' I whisper.

'What did?'

'When I . . . *exploded*. When I just let rip, didn't think, just let the words shoot out of me...it felt good.'

There's a pause. Jill's waiting to see if I've finished talking. She always does that — it's really nice, because most people can't wait to jump in and interrupt.

'The way I see it,' she says gently, 'you were like a pressure cooker with the lid on tight. And the pressure built and built, until it was unbearable. And then — you literally blew your top. *Boom*.'

I laugh, sniffing.

'Of course it feels good, when that happens,' she says. 'It feels great. All that horrible pressure gone. But then it starts to build up again.'

I nod. I know she's right.

'And it takes so much energy just to keep the lid held down, just to keep the fear and unhappiness down...'

'I know,' I whisper. 'It feels that way.'

'Why don't you let it out gradually, bit by bit?' she asks, gently. 'Instead of waiting till it builds up so much it bursts out?'

'How?' I croak.

'Well — that's partly what these sessions are about. Letting everything out into the open, taking a good look at it, seeing that it's not really that scary after all.'

I nod, because I have started to feel better over the last week or so. I've started to feel less afraid.

'Think of all the energy you'll save, not keeping that lid clamped down,' she goes on. 'Haven't you got better things to do with that energy?'

At the beginning of March, I try to give up my pills completely, but I feel so bad I go back on them again. Just a low dose, though.

178

One day, soon after that, Mum comes into my room and I know from her face she's got something serious to tell me. She announces she's got the papers through for her and Dad to get a divorce. It's easy to do, apparently, because of Anita.

I ask her how she can talk about Anita and the divorce so calmly, although I feel pretty calm too, somehow. And she says: 'Look – I can't blame her, Fliss. Our marriage was finished anyway. Over a year ago – two, maybe. But we just drifted along until Anita came on the scene. And that heated everything up. It made your dad desperate to walk out . . . but we would've split up anyway. I'm sure of that.'

And then she just stays, sitting on the end of my bed, and we chat about how she's doing without Dad and how I'm getting on in my sessions with Jill and everything. Then suddenly she tells me she's sorry. She says she was so worried about the girls she forgot I needed help too and she tried to lean on me like I was an adult, and that wasn't fair. When she says that, I start crying. It's weird, I don't make any sound, but these streams of water run from my eyes, and I'm gulping a bit and she puts her arms round me and just holds me. After that she goes downstairs and makes some tea, and when she comes up again we're a bit awkward together, but very warm, somehow. She says, 'It's my birthday soon.'

'I know,' I say.

'Let's have a party, Fliss. Just a little one. I'll ask Jan, maybe, but it'll just be us five and we can have a big cream cake and cheap champagne and a good old laugh, ay?'

'Done,' I say.

'Great. Maybe I'll let the girls ask a friend each. You know – stop them squabbling.'

'Yeah, why not.'

'But then you'll be the only one without a friend. D'you want to ask Liz?'

'I can't ask Liz and not Megan.'

'Well − ask her too. Why not. We'll have a real girls' night. I ought to cook though, if there's that many − I could do lasagne or − why're you laughing at me?'

'Cos it's turning into a real party, isn't it? Like the old days. You used to love parties.'

And her eyes go all wet, and she says, 'Yeah, I know. I still do.'

A few days after that, I stop the pills completely. And a few days after that, I realize I've stopped feeling like someone looking on at what's going on in the family, I've become part of it again. I have a big row with Alexa about her using my make-up. I tell Mum she shouldn't drink so much, although I'm not really worried about her, not any more. And then a week after that, I'm back in school.

My form tutor's brilliant, he's a real support. I never had much to do with him before but that's because I never needed to. He goes over with me what I've got to do to catch up, but says I mustn't feel at all pressured. He tells me the sixth-form college will make allowances for what he calls my 'troubles', and go on my predicted GCSE grades if necessary. He tells me not to worry if I need a day off now and then − just to take it. I feel he's really on my side.

He does something else for me. He puts me in touch with Melissa. She's in the other half of our year and I only know her by sight. My form tutor asks her to speak to me about the whole thing of being in a divided family.

She pitches up alongside me one lunchtime and says, 'I dunno. Just cos I gave this stunning speech in the debating group about the benefits of having two families everyone sees me as some kind of expert.'

At first I think that's a pretty big-headed thing to say, but she has such a comical, long-suffering look on her face as she says it that I laugh, and she laughs too, and asks, straight out, 'You met the other woman yet?'

I shake my head, croak, 'Only once. I can't ... I can't imagine just being in a room with her, just chatting to her and stuff.'

'That's normal,' says Melissa. 'Totally normal. It took me *ages* to agree to meet my dad's new wife. I used to jam my hands over my ears when he tried to talk to me about her. And I wouldn't go to the wedding.'

'How old were you?'

'Fourteen. Real vicious age, right? Felt I had to side with my mum. Then Mum met someone new, only a year later. And that really took the pressure off and now – I like my new stepmum. Better than my mum's boyfriend, really. So I spend quite a bit of time over there.'

I gawp at her. She makes it sound so easy, so simple. I think it's like she's finished this long journey, one that I'm right at the start of.

'My stepmum's Spanish,' Melissa goes on. 'And her English is like – basic, and right between the eyes sometimes. I'm convinced that made things easier, you know? We had to be direct with each other – straight with each other. The first time I met her, I went over there for lunch. And she'd gone to such huge trouble, just for me – you had to like her for it. Then – at the end of it – Dad disappeared off upstairs. They must've had it planned. I was just feeling a bit shirty, a bit uneasy, when she opened up this huge box of chocs and shoved it at me and said, "Look, let's get this over with. I'm not in competition with you for your dad. We have different things with him. He and I have stuff that would put him behind bars if he had that with you."'

'Blimey! She just came out with it?'

'Yup. "You and your dad," she said, "you share the same blood. Nothing'll change that. His relationship with me might die, but you're his daughter for ever. He'd die for you. He wouldn't die for me and I don't want him to because he's got you to think of. So let's not have any jealousy crap, OK?" And then she stood up and came round the table and put her arms round me and just about squeezed the life out of me.'

'Wow. Did it work?'

'What she said? Yeah. Somehow. And it's not just words, with her. She's always on about how important it is if you have the same blood. She's dead intense about family. She gives Dad shit if he's not around for my birthday and stuff. She goes ballistic – "What kind of father are you?" And I quite like it that she's so physical. I mean – she comes up and hugs you, whether you want her to or not, but even if you don't want her to it's nice, in a way. I used to think she was a bit dim, cos she didn't recognise the signals people sent out, but I've changed my mind. She does know what moods people are in but she just rides over them, turns them around – she's good enough to do that. She gets you on her side.'

'Not all the time?'

'No. 'Course not. Sometimes I just scream at her to

sod off, and she does sod off, and she takes it all in her stride and doesn't sulk. She's – clever. She does this jokey thing of ganging up with me against Dad, sometimes. Tells him to give me a bigger allowance and stuff. So I can *live well*. She's always on about living well. And then we both start taking the piss out of Dad and she shouts and waves her arms about – it's hilarious, he loves it, we end up in fits.'

'He *likes* being yelled at?'

'Yeah, but it's different. It's a game, and he knows it. You ever seen flamenco?'

I shake my head. 'Only in that old dance film, what was it called . . .'

'Dunno. Nuria says one of the things in flamenco is making a dance out of the way men and women are so different, and how they fight. They shout and challenge each other in flamenco, and then it's out of their system and they're getting on again. Dad says she's going all flamenco on him when she starts leading off. See – there's this Spanish idea that you shout at someone when you really care about them, when you care enough to be upset by them.'

'I didn't think flamenco was about fighting – I thought it was about sex.'

Melissa looks at me, all wry. 'It's all in there together. But let's not go there – he's still my *dad*.'

I see Melissa on and off quite a bit after that. We bump into each other at school, end up talking. She tells me about her new baby stepbrother, how she thought she'd be jealous but she loves him. She tells me about how Nuria's family are always turning up to stay and how great they are, especially Nuria's eighteen-year-old male cousin who's very fit and always after her to practise his English on.

I think a lot about what Nuria said – about how Melissa's dad would die for her. I'm not sure my dad would die for me, but he is making more of an effort. Whenever he turns up to take the girls off to the cinema or somewhere, he always comes up to my room to say hello and ask how I am. It's a bit wooden, a bit embarrassing, but at least he does it. Then one night he rings and arranges to take me out for dinner, just me. It's to a really posh restaurant and I feel quite nervous and excited about it, but then he blows it all the next night by phoning and asking if I'd like Anita to come along too. I can't speak when he does that, I just put the phone down on him. And then when Mum finds me in my room crying and gets the story out of me she stamps off straight away and I can hear her yelling at him down the phone.

He waits two days, then he phones back. He says he's sorry, he was insensitive, and will I still go out to eat with him? I do, and the restaurant and the food are fantastic but it's been spoilt, somehow. It's like Anita's sitting there with us anyway.

The GCSEs get closer, but I feel far less nervous than I thought I'd be. I've discovered something. When you've been right down, really down and destroyed, and you manage to get yourself up again – you're stronger for it everywhere.

Twenty-eight

I'm still seeing Jill, but only once a week now. I have good and bad weeks, I have good and bad sessions. One day I'm feeling really low and Jill can't get me to talk much. 'Doesn't it get depressing?' I ask her, sourly. 'Talking about people's troubles all the time?'

She shakes her head. 'Actually, I find it inspirational.'

'You do?' I scoff.

'Yes. You kids, dealing with trauma, all kinds of trauma – most of you are so brave. So – resourceful. You're against these awful odds, but you still come out the other end.'

I smile weakly. 'I don't feel I'm coming out the other end.'

'Not yet maybe. Not quite. But you will, you'll make it. You're getting there. I can tell, just by the way you talk.'

I feel this rush of tears, when she says that, and I look down, sniffing. She reaches into the box of tissues, pulls one out, and hands it to me. Then she says: 'Well, Fliss, since you're not going to do much talking today, I'm afraid I'm going to tell you my bay tree story.'

'What?'

'My bay tree story. It's a true story. I'm in it.'

I smile. 'Go on then.'

'My dad – he's a widower. Mum died ten years ago.'

I think about saying I'm sorry, but before I can, she goes on: 'I don't see him as often as I ought to. He lives quite a long way away. He's OK, though. He's got his own house and good neighbours, and a lovely little garden. He loves gardening. There's a patio, too, but it looks awful – bare, empty. I kept on at him to buy some flowerpots but he said they were too fiddly. So, one Christmas, I bought him this lovely big terracotta pot with a little bay tree in it. I told him it was for the patio and he was delighted. But the next time I went round, it wasn't on the patio. The old bugger had stood it down in the garden, on the edge of the grass.'

I laugh, and she goes on, 'I ticked him off, of course. And he just said – it looked so lonely, stuck up on the paved bit, that he shifted it down with the other plants. Plants like company, he said.'

She stops, takes a drink of water, and I'm just wondering whether this is the point of the story, all about plants being like people needing company, when she says, 'My dad really can't relate to growing things in pots. I bought him food for the bay tree, you know, fertiliser, but he forgot to feed it. And it hardly grew, and its leaves were all pale – it looked really sickly, awful. I kept nagging him and I'd feed it whenever I was there. Then there was a time one spring when I was very busy and I didn't see him for a while – two months maybe. The next time I visited I went out into the garden and there was the bay tree, *transformed*. Twice, three times its old size. It looked absolutely glorious – all green and lush and healthy, wonderful. So I said: "Well done, Dad! You started feeding it at last!" And he looked all kind of sheepish and said: "No I didn't. You try and shift that pot." So I did, and I couldn't. It was stuck fast. A couple of roots from the tree had found their way through the hole in the bottom of the pot, and gone deep into the ground, and got nourishment that way. That was all it took: all it needed.'

There's a pause. Then she grins at me and says, 'Sometimes kids come back and see me, tell me they've sorted themselves out. It is totally brilliant to see them, looking all clear-eyed and positive. And I always think of the time I walked into Dad's garden and saw the bay tree, all the odds against it, fighting its way through that tiny hole in the bottom of the pot, looking all glossy and strong and brilliant.'

'What if it hadn't though?' I mutter.

'What?'

'Fought its way out?'

'It would've died, I guess. The point is, it did fight. It wasn't fair it had to, it wasn't fair it wasn't planted straight in the ground, or fed in the pot, but it battled its way through. It got it sorted. Just like all the kids I see who have everything stacked against them, but they still find a life. Just like you're going to do.'

There's a pause, then I ask, 'What's it like now?'

'The bay tree? Fantastic. Taller than me. Dad left it in the same place, even though it throws out the rest of the garden a bit.' She looks straight at me and grins. 'It cracked the pot wide open years ago.'

What the judges and media have said about Livewire

Livewire Books have won:

The Other Award
The Red Fist and Silver Slate Pencil Award
The Council on Interracial Books Award
The National Conference of Christians and
Jews Mass Media Award
The Lewis Carroll Shelf Award

and much, much more.

The press has said:

'Outstanding' *Vogue*
'Stupendous' *Guardian*
'Outrageously funny' *7 Days*
'Hugely enjoyable' *British Book News*
'Compulsively witty' *Times Literary Supplement*
'Riotous and down-to-earth' *Africa World Review*
'Genuinely funny' *Los Angeles Times*
'Explosive . . . exceptional' *Times Literary Supplement*
'Brilliant' *Observer*
'Riotous' *Times Educational Supplement*

The bestselling Coll and Art trilogy . . .

Kate Cann
Diving In

'As the hot water pounded down on me I was suddenly aware
that I was not alone. Someone was standing very close to me,
under the same shower. I opened my eyes, blinking away
water. It was him . . . '

Colette daydreams all the time about meeting the gorgeous
bloke she sees at her local swimming pool. Then, one afternoon,
he asks her out. Close-up, he's even more good-looking – but
he's also very pushy.

As Coll struggles to get what *she* wants from their relationship,
she begins to wonder just how far she should go. Can she cope
with a boyfriend who's much more experienced than her? How
much should she suppress what she's increasingly feeling? Will
she turn out like her man-hating mum – or like Art's sad last
girlfriend who suddenly got dumped? Just how fast should Coll
be diving into love?

Fiction £5.99
ISBN 0 7043 4980 9

Kate Cann
In the Deep End

Coll has *just* about forgiven Art for assuming that she will sleep
with him when they're away with his parents for the weekend.
But the Big Question still looms. Art wants and expects sex –
and Coll wants it too. It's not a matter of 'if' any more, more of
when and where.

Then they do take the plunge and Coll finds herself caught up in
a welter of new emotions. In the midst of powerful and exciting
sexual feelings, Coll must keep her life afloat. Juggling exams,
commitments to friends, *and* trying to get Art to talk about
what's happening with him, Coll soon finds out that she is now
well and truly in the deep end.

Fiction £5.99
ISBN 0 7043 4981 7

Kate Cann
Sink or Swim

When Coll first fancied Art from afar, she had no idea that they
would soon be involved in a stormy but passionate relationship.
Now, they have broken painfully apart. Coll is determined to get
on with her life, but getting Art out of her mind proves harder
than she thought.

Before long, her family and friends are losing their patience with
her, and, when Art suddenly reappears on the scene, Coll finds
she has a difficult decision to make. As she struggles in a
whirlpool of anger, distress, logic and longing, Coll knows that
she must choose whether to sink – or to strike out for the shore.

Fiction £5.99
ISBN 0 7043 4982 5

. . . and so do her readers.

'Fantastic. I have read all the books in the Coll and Art series and they are all fab' Billie, Norfolk

'If you read the first you just HAVE to read the second and third!' Stephanie, Dorset

'Absolutely brilliant' Claire, Dublin

'It was almost like reading my own life' Jean, Nottingham

'When you've finished you want to read them all over again!' Alex, Cardiff

'The Coll and Art series are the best books I have ever read' Heather, Lancashire

'These are those "I can't stop reading" books' Amy, Inverness

'Fantastic – so true to life. These books made me angry, and also made me laugh and cry' Jo, Devon

'I couldn't put the books down they were so good . . . I have just got to find out what happens with Coll and Art' Sara, Cornwall